MR DINEEN'S CAREFUL PARADE

T0164528

THOMAS McCARTHY

Mr Dineen's Careful Parade

NEW AND SELECTED POEMS

ANVIL PRESS POETRY

Published in 1999
by Anvil Press Poetry Ltd
Neptune House 70 Royal Hill London SE10 8RF

Copyright © Thomas McCarthy 1999

ISBN 0 85646 320 5

This book is published
with financial assistance from
The Arts Council of England

A catalogue record for this book
is available from the British Library

The moral rights of the author have been asserted in
accordance with the Copyright, Designs and Patents Act 1988

Designed and set in Monotype Ehrhardt by Anvil
Printed and bound in England
by Cromwell Press, Trowbridge, Wiltshire

*for Catherine
and for Kate Inez and Neil*

ACKNOWLEDGEMENTS

Acknowledgements are due to the following which first published the work: *Ambit, Belfast Review, Cyphers, Eire-Ireland, The Holly Bough* (Examiner Publications, Cork), *The Honest Ulsterman, The Iowa Review, The Irish Times*, Minnesota Public Radio, Monitor Radio, *New Statesman, Nua (USA), Poetry* (Chicago), *Poetry Ireland Review, Princeton University Library Chronicle*, RTE One Television, RTE Radio One, *Rhinoceros* (Belfast), *Southern Review* and *The Sunday Independent* (Poems of the Month).

The author gratefully acknowledges the assistance of the Arts Council, Dublin, for bursaries in 1979 and 1989, and of the American-Irish Foundation in 1984. Thanks are also due to the Irish American Cultural Institute in New Jersey and the Center for Irish Studies at the University of St. Thomas, especially to Tom Redshaw and Jim Rogers.

CONTENTS

New Poems

FROM *The First Convention* (1978)

FROM *Seven Winters in Paris* (1989)

New Poems

PATRICK STREET

Today, the passionate light of a city in the South,
                                   red light
of October and its various shades. Sunlight
                                 in a passing car
like a stunned moth on a theatre poster:
                                 the heartbeat
of what has happened here and what's to come.

GRAND PARADE

Lights change in the street of the yellow horse.
                                 Green turns
to red and keeps us waiting. We must
                                 wait in line
as centuries waited in line to be tossed
                                 into a river.
Orange and green. Lovers lean against a light.

ROCHESTOWN ROAD

The lights of Rochestown from my study window;
                                a bourgeois
infestation from the boarding schools of the West.
                                September of '64
and '65 and 1969, gymslips and football boots
                                all wedded now.
Their adult lives, like ragwort, yellow in the rain.

MONTENOTTE

Suburb of the leaking roof and the saturated
                                cornice:
the city looks in at us through damaged windows.
                                Shutters and cloud
are opened. October threatens more sunlight
                                to bake again
our exhausted walls, the folded-down valerian.

UNIVERSITY COLLEGE

After the wrought-iron gate, wrought-iron bridge,
                                        I wander
through the undergrowth of laurel and camellia.
                                        In truth,
afraid. I fear that twenty-year-old revisionist:
                                the second-year
I was, the cool bitterness. My own *dépit amoureux*.

SWANS AT THE NMRC

Swans glide on the Lee near the Electronics Centre,
                                their heads bowed
like young engineers, or priests, over the sacred wafer
                                of microchips.
One breaks the surface with its beak, one adjusts
                                the wayward printout
of cygnets. Science flows between fax and surplice.

FRENCH CHURCH STREET

We go the way of all Huguenots tonight.
      The street's on fire
with the red glow of October. Unexpected light
        follows us
like a foreign skill with cloth. Red sails
      of early evening
tack homeward. The very stars are Huguenot.

WATERSTONE'S, SATURDAY NIGHT

We read the elemental *Odes* of Pablo Neruda,
       five poets
of the South. In my old book, a press-cutting
      of Santiago station.
Chile so far away, only rain with seven names,
      our unhoping song,
weeps upon the windows of Patrick Street.

BLACKROCK CASTLE

Kitsch it was then, kitsch as any castle
                              praised in song.
It stands by the river, dead drunk now
                              in a new suit.
But its floodlights from the roundabout
                              meant I'd escaped
yet again the congested flood-plain.

TIVOLI ROUNDABOUT

A three-car pile-up on a Saturday night:
                              blue lights
of a squad car, and the smoky blue haze
                              of Montenotte
is my mirror from the traffic of childhood.
                    I must stall
with this blue night on the roundabout.

PÉGUY

At the heart of France, such divine Grace.
You, Charles Péguy, you thirst
For a deep and mysterious victory,

A meadow in high summer, the Île de France.
There, the sun shines on your childhood battalions:
Bergson, Pascal, Corneille, St Joan.

GREAT VOYAGER

for Dervla Murphy

When the Chinese discovered Europe
They robbed no gold;
Nor did they make covenants of blood –

Instead, Chang Ch'ien
Took home the alfalfa and grapevine.
He already owned the rose.

DENG XIAOPING

1904–1997

When you were a young Wolfe Tone in Paris
You looked like the fashionable Jacobin,
Your stare an inscrutable *Jail Journal*,

But the photographer's carpet at your feet
Held all the promise of *Four Modernizations*.
Set sail, now, against Bantry and Kuomintang.

LOUIS MacNEICE IN AMERICA

Your *Autumn Journal* is still in my hand
as I leave Grennan's Vassar. A cinnamon roll
crumbles when I find your imaginary islands,
Marlborough and Achill. The train edges
apologetically across the marshalling-yard
of the Hudson. Coffee stains your stanzas.

It is your voice more than any other
that I hear on my Amtrak journeys.
In Plattsburg, New York State,
a teenager flirts with a tired conductor:
Sir, do you think I'm a slut? I'm psychosexual!
The narrator in you would make a poem of this,
for you were the poet of the damaged.

Beside me a priest fears for the Berlin wall,
a professor fears for the life of the Pope,
an illegal immigrant fears for Ireland.
How you would have connected all
these things, as you connected friends
with their fulfilled and unfulfilled hopes.

While there's life and cigarettes there's hope.
Sanguine heart, you described hope without faith;
blessed particulars without God or Lenin;
life highly glossed like lipstick on a cup
                    or the rim of a glass.
How quickly you understood there was less sin
in America than in any other place.

NEW AGE TRAVELLERS AT COOLNASMUTAWN

Broken-down against a bleak wall of bare trees,
their van floats, leaf-like, on a pond of mud.
It is December in Glenshelane Wood,
cold comfort in a bleak afternoon of mist.
I watch the blue ribbon of woodsmoke,
whippets and alsatians scratching at a number-plate,
children running free while days deteriorate.

Here great red salmon leap four feet out of spray,
getting further inland. Salmon's mystical need
to return to where it all began
seems like this family in a Bradford bread-van.
Both struggle with water at the weir of Europe,
unable to get further West. They voyage, untidy, quiet,
like charcoal-burners out of Raleigh's estate.

But this time round, instead of wild Condons,
they find Anne at their hatch with turkey and sauce
on Christmas Eve, my cousin John with cooked beef.
They open slowly like a garrison, suddenly pleased,
and say: 'Sorry, luv, we're all vegetarians 'ere.'
They take the Brussels sprouts from Anne's hand;
and John, happy, intimate with a girl from England.

Generosity is simple still, the State complex:
there's no escape from the voteless Commission.
The writ of Europe runs, even in this wood.
Within days Caesar's troops will restore the solitude
our native middle-class enjoy. The simple countryman
is hurrying on to cash his Headage Payment cheques.
Pity him, he grows codicils instead of food.

Welcome, happy to take advantage since the Land
Acts of long ago. Welcome to the refuge of trees,
the ancient alphabet, dinnseanchas, the pipers' reeds,
the Enya attitude that milks the foreigner.
New Age Traveller, refugee from Leeds, understand
if you seek refuge in this salmon-rich forest
you head for spawn beds as hostile as the next.

THE MUSICIAN'S LOVE-NEST

for Catherine

White dust of summer on white paint
and late evening sun through the skylight:
the world was in its youth when we came
to Sydney Place. We climbed to the light
of Number 6. Oh, so frantic with hope.
Books and potatoes in their jackets,
a sugar-bowl in the cooling cupboard;
together we watched the stove perspire.
What more could we do to squeeze more life,
what could we do, love, with so much desire?

Each night, just for a laugh, we lit the fire
or cooked a cautious meal for Sara and Seán.
Two of us were reading Douglas D. on ratatouille.
St Kilda's Parliament was our skinny cookbook.
We lived in a neighbourhood that loved Seán Dunne.
Each day he was brought love in spoonfuls
to keep and cook. His laughter like butterscotch
grew hard, sweet, brittle with little time to write.
His clothes were a theatre under jet-black hair.
His voice like Joyce, a shade of early death.

But these rooms, truly, were our own space.
In them our hopes were hung aloft, like huge
paper lamp-shades, towering in their wattage.
Years went by, paper of delicate shades,
drenched and bright in astonishing marriage.
My head was the space that love had rented.
Looking into the bright room, I heard music,
Czech music, piano of Martinů and Janaček.
It had the feel of a musicians' love-nest,
Jan Cap and his beloved, Cork and Prague.

Those days being personal were most in touch
with everything that happens. White dust
of summer on white paint was immediate, white
with intimacy as if without a language.
Love's bloom was on the ivory of each hour –
skylight sun on the brilliant Steinway
of each new day; Sunday evenings
and the smell from stews your mother cooked.
Sure, time plays tricks and edits everything,
but I believe in the space controlled by love,
charism of memory, redemptive dust of poems.

KATE INEZ, THE MOON AND STARS

This night, your birthday. You come out to look
at the moon. The night is clear and sharp.
From the lintel of our earth
you take the springtime bearings. You work,

like Aristarchos of Samos, by gifts alone
to balance a telescope at the door.
The moon is full, the fragile sun long gone
with Herakleitos' miserly one third of a metre.

Because you are my daughter the stars are still
just where they fed your brother, Herakles –
one hundred thousand million stars,
galactic fog, a Catherine wheel of galaxies.

A flash of light, six hundred million miles an hour,
reflects off your silver-coated lens:
this week of your eleventh birthday
it is a metaphor, direct as Newgrange.

It collates all the cool mysteries of being young,
that's what it does; the way Orbiter and Luna
collated the moon, or the way Mariner and Voyager
probed the outer planets. None could know that

all the elements of a voyage are left at home.
Always only the hardware is sent into space –
even Valery Ryumin had to return
to talk of his three hundred and sixty two days.

It is the stars, in fact, dear Kate Inez,
that are constant in their probe towards you.
It's the moon that wants to bring you into focus,
thereby getting warmth, becoming renewed

and humane at the edge of nothingness.
So as you fret and worry at angles
it is the moon and her sister stars
that want to voyage earthwards to your heart.

You are the prefect of their night sky,
on the nursing chair of earth, the goddess Hera
whose steadfast elegance stands by
us all. Headlong into the interior

the star-ships and lunar-modules come.
On your birthday, the rearranged stars
and all their moons fill your new telescope;
you their destiny, Kepler, Galileo, daughter.

ST PATRICK'S DAY WITH NEIL

We start this day in an embarrassment of March,
St Patrick's Day. My wide-awake displeasure
is not of interest to you. After a year
in the US you think Bill Clinton is Taoiseach.
You still hope for the yellow truck from Schwans.
What is your nation? It's still unclear.
Are you for Cork or the Minnesota *Twins*?
Don't decide, not on this day of green beer

and things gone haywire for the umpteenth time.
You lie in our bed for comfort and praise,
the fresh weave of a blanket on your delicate face.
St Patrick's Day in bed with the radio on.
Their public façade, their *cupla focail*. Your turtle-
head clears the eiderdown. You wait for the storm
of rain that always comes; then leave the place
of refuge abruptly. We're the rejected Church

and watch you leap across the shaggy room.
St Patrick's Day begins in kilts of heavy rain.
You were first to hear the pluralist hailstorm
and the noise of life beyond the eiderdown.
And there you speed, hero of daylight,
head forward into the day's Fontenoy:
the battle is yours, brilliant, irredentist boy.
No panel on the radio could get this right –

how one small boy in his native country
(Prince William at Eton, Sheridan Lowell in Mass.)
can define completely his parents' place.
I rise and follow you to better see
what you make of the drenched and native earth:
only to find you before me at the kitchen door
laughing with the daft warmth of a Celt,
your plastic beaker held aloft in the downpour.

This day you carry with an air of confidence.
I know it's because you've something hoarded,
a cup full of hailstones in the freezer,
salted away like a trust fund offshore.
I watch you, bare-headed in a teeshirt,
holding the blue beaker to a bountiful sky.
The grey hail of St Patrick's Day
bounces like nuts of wisdom on your head.

The freezer, then, has a kind of inner knowledge
that you have rights over. I can understand
from my own boyhood the strength of a hoard.
I hid coins and copies of the *Hotspur*
from enemies of boys. My hoard was concealed.
The loose brick in Nanna's wall had a Swiss number.
But I never had the audacity to hide, like you,
the mysteries of weather, a hoard of hail.

A DINER ON CONCORDIA

IN MEMORY OF ROGER BLAKELY

> *It was a hard thing to leave that creek, one of*
> *the hardest things we ever did, but we had all*
> *the trout we wished and the rest could wait.*
>
> SIGURD F. OLSON

A pan fizzes in the ordinary speech
of Minnesota. The diner on Concordia
has grown quiet. Only you and Bill Truesdale
and a pile of books have breakfast.
A waitress gaffs the morning checks,
so many fish on the aluminium spike.

What's a city for if not for breakfast?
A winter place for writing summers down,
a neighbourhood greasy spoon
where you can snow-shoe across photos
of the North Shore: a diner is where
the incidents of our myth are netted.

Grab a menu. I take hold
of one table corner and feel the strain:
so many coffees kick against me,
fresh toast leaps away, cream escapes.
You and Bill are old hands at this,
memory and breakfast, netting the fish.

Roger, I am grateful for your patience,
being a 'rookie', as you Americans say,
when it comes to breakfast. Remembrance,
though, is one of my national arts.
We contrast County Kerry with the North Shore,
compare busy Duluth to the port of Cork,

and agree to come here when the snow settles –
for snow is the nest, the instinct of Minnesota,
snow is the badger's set, the shimmering pool
where edibles have accumulated.
Roger, you were the life-long fisher,
a Professor of the lakes and prairies:

a *courrier du bois* or *voyageur*
hauling knowledge across the between-lands;
Ojibwa creeks, Finnish lakes, Swedish towns.
Snow falls on the Mozart gas-station.
When you speak trout leap from Schubert,
a dressed fly falls across a quintet.

SOME HIDDEN TREES

Because I've no father to watch raking leaves,
I come to your September garden.
My car crackles on abandoned gold-leaf
as I cross the cut-stone bridge at Lismore,
enter once more that pleasant commonwealth
of Big House and cross-roads. West Waterford
is beautiful in its reductive leaf-mould
where trees have shed their loose binding.

I shed a world where politics is rotten –
enemies acting as if for the first time
they find they hate each other.
I return to a September luxury
of seed and leaf, a garden in the South
where malice is lowered to a pH level
below the grief of summer. The march-past
ends here in a cul-de-sac of compost.

I pass by an encumbered language:
once more, *we dwelleth in Mounster*
where politics stays at the high hedge,
weary and necessary as the equinox.
Autumn halts things with its abundance,
makes conversation in a feckless country.
Leaf and wind, and strong kinship

between us is my seasonal respite.
It keeps the spirits well, the paths clear.
We debrief each other as we pace the grass
until halted by senators of nettle and briar.
We come upon an abandoned corner,
DHF and I, and wonder if apples
still grow upon some hidden trees.
I crash through brambles like an Army sapper,
spade in one hand, bucket in the other,

to find abundant apples in a cloud
of blackberries: such entanglement
of abundance I knew about since childhood.
I set to work in my own clearing,
Denis anxiously calling at the fringe of things –
but myself at work like an only son;
picking off the fruit of Raleigh and Spenser,
beyond the politics of my anxious youth.

AMARANTHUS

IN MEMORY OF SEÁN DUNNE AND MOLLY KEANE

Bid Amaranthus all his beauty shed – LYCIDAS

It is months since I heard the sound of rain.
April throws its glassy grains of sand
and I take notice. At long last
I look out on life, its throwing hand
still raised in anger at our inattention.
The sun turns its face away in wet disgust,
as it grieves with our life in this life.
I barely occupy the space that power allocates,
but spill the talent, memory, into negative earth.
Somewhere there is an atmosphere for our kind of work.

Out of a Waterford childhood, the swinging gate
has a boy upon it. This remembered life,
it contains already the scattered family:
beloved names, Molly Keane, Seán Dunne,
who move behind the black embroidery of April.
I wait for them to speak after heavy rain,
but they too find heaven inarticulate inside.
Their 1980s sit upon my white window-sill

with them inside that decade. Sit beside me,
Seán. Gauge the antics of dissatisfied life.
A motor stalls at Cappoquin House, a poet
stalls upon a Quaker meeting-place.
By contemplation, Molly, images break free:
in Ardmore learn widowhood, cup by cup.

Memory is the mother of our widowhood,
forever threatened, bearer of message-bags
on a high bicycle. Memory knows
who to touch for help, and when to economize
with truth. The space we occupy makes sense
only when it speaks. Make death's acquaintance,

meet the ideal flower, pollen of memory,
that colours the graves of our cemetery within.
We are not lightened by the friends we shed –
as in drowned Lycidas, that old Republican
made immortal garlands. Flowers never fade
there. They scent all the dead we carry.

So rain on the glass is unfaded flower.
Seán, this is the Cork rain we shared for years;
and you, Molly Keane, you are stilled in a grove
of troublesome novels. Themes are not like hips,
to be replaced. It is right to hold a steady gaze
like amaranthus, memory, or the poet Dunne.

THE CAPPOQUIN CRICKET XI

Memory is a *plein air* studio,
contemporaneous, ourselves looking on:
like this Edwardian afternoon in Cappoquin.
It is a resolute moment above our town,
a game of cricket ended. Eleven men
kneel down awhile before letting go.

Young men, no doubt, from the best families
                              of my native town,
the top eleven of the freehold name-plates.
Each one is at ease with the photographer
twelve years before the Free State
made such self-assurance legitimate:

Frahers, Oldens and Whites, Collenders
and Walshes, a young Kenny from the square,
Laceys born to be factory managers,
Barrons and Currans, Bolgers and Sargents.
Boarding-schools and monsignor uncles
will uplift the more banal trades.

Here we find the past at its most naked,
men fully dressed in cricket whites, prosperous,
not an Ireland to be imagined or made
whole in national speeches, but the thing itself:
social power and its immortal oneness
as well-connected as a Diocesan priest.

One player with flowing black curls
and perfect smiling teeth, he'll inherit
an import business and a river boat.
A youth with eyes and mouth that never smile
will make his fortune as a Sweepstake agent.
None of them, as far as I can tell,
will lose in love; none will marry a local.

Connections will be made from other towns.
Middle-class in a poor, congested land,
their destinies seem relentless, destined.
A nation awake, soviets and flying columns,
to the very end nothing disturbs the pattern.
Bourgeois chances were theirs to take

on afternoons never as tendentious
as my own bitter speculation is.
Words are things I hurl from Twig Bog Lane.
They stick for a moment to such perfect ease:
a simple photograph, the white comfort
of sport. Only, my childhood is a jealous critic
and burns the plate at their bended knees.

FROM

The First Convention

STRANGER, HUSBAND

Strange he seemed to her dark
eyes; strange, his lack of interest,

his incessant breaking of wood.
His every swing seemed blessed

in its fruitfulness: a broad
spray of chippings covered the

ground like a net, catching split
wood, cupping it within his range.

What would happen, she thought, what
would the dark-haired working-man
do if I dared the first approach?

There was the sound of an axe finding
rest in wood, touching equilibrium
when she entered his place of work.

STATE FUNERAL

Parnell will never come again, he said. He's there,
all that was mortalof him. Peace to his ashes

JAMES JOYCE: *Ulysses*

That September afternoon the family
Gathered. There was a native *déjà vu*
Of Funeral when we settled against the couch
On our sunburnt knees. We gripped mugs of tea
Tightly and soaked the TV spectacle;
The boxed ritual in our living-room.

My father recited prayers of memory,
Of monster meetings, blazing tar-barrels
Planted outside Free-State homes, the Broy-
Harriers pushing through a crowd, Blueshirts;
And, after the war, De Valera's words
Making Churchill's imperial palette blur.

What I remember is one decade of darkness,
A mind-stifling boredom; long summers
For blackberry picking and churning cream,
Winters for saving timber or setting lines
And snares: none of the joys of here and now
With its instant jam, instant heat and cream:

It was a landscape for old men. Today
They lowered the tallest one, tidied him
Away while his people watched quietly.
In the end he had retreated to the first dream,
Caning truth. I think of his austere grandeur;
Taut sadness, like old heroes he had imagined.

THE FIRST CONVENTION

I

I wanted to be up front where I could
see the headlights piercing the darkness,
where I could follow the curving line
of the road whitening before the lights;
where I could see phantom patches
of fog, opening and rising upward like

lace curtains fluttering at an open window
I scrambled into the passenger-seat, gripping
the dashboard with my small hands to raise
my body into the fullness of the lights.
Satisfied, nose pressed against the wind-
screen, I relived the night's activities.

II

That scene returns in dream: rough-coated men
waving white polling cards, shouting 'Yes' or
'No' as the questions ooze from the speakers;
and the huge brown buttons on their over-
coats scratching my face, closing me in: the
thick smell of beer and sweat nauseating.

Always I force an opening to the doorway,
through the excited mass of polling cards.
In my dream-garden I can hear their faded
oratory, the dying crackle of applause;
the force of national politics soft-
ening in the huge quietness of the dark.

GREATRAKES, THE HEALER

He himself tells us that an inward inspiration informed him
he had the gift . . . which persuasion grew so strong that he
touched several persons and fully cured them.

SMITH'S *Waterford*, 1745

His was a landscape of wounds and disease;
the women crying at his gate-lodge had
collapsed into skin and bone; bone itself
might have hosted some terminal disease;
their children playing together had seen
the scab of death break frequently and bleed.

On summer days he had to flee the riot
of sufferers gathering at his windows,
screaming through the iron bars, their
eyes blown into bulbs of expectation:
then he would run to the stable and mount
the fastest hunter to flee from his gift.

On days when the gift took control he would
be pulled into its tight ritual of healing;
he would chant Ease and Health into sick
bodies, reinstating balance with his touch–
But later his calls to cure became less
frequent; spasms of doubt had sapped the will

Of the suffering peasantry. Dying will-
power caused a collective lethargy.
Unwilling to be cured, they died quietly
in smoke-filled cottages. From the roadway
he saw them. Too many wounds, making Faith-
Healing seem a neutral, pathetic act.

MARIE, MARIE

I remember her soft face,
the bright eyes, when coaxed,
splintering into laughter

and her white, ringed fingers
clutching a world of books.

I remember the white
mornings of January, and Marie,
mufflered and gloved, humming
a dance-hall tune:

in the evenings she would
retrace her singing-path,
carrying the same whiteness
back to Belleville.

Months later I saw her singing-
face under a Sunday headline:
her body lay collapsed like
a rag-doll against a city wall:

all I could feel of that warm break-
fast was a singing numbness,
white memories turned red with
grief; grief emptying into loss.

BREAKING GARDEN

He's reluctant to move; old campaigner
Familiar with siege. He had spent hours
On violent streets during the 'thirties,
Refusing to move despite batons and gas:
But this is the year of forced migration;
Letters, books are stuffed in bags like grain,
Pictures and paperweights, crumbling squadrons
Of files await the retreating campaign.

Patricia's more resigned. Quiet in acquiescence:
She moves quickly between rows of growth,
Deciding which plants must stay. I watched her
For days. With two sheepdogs for lieutenants
She tested the tallest stems; made a note
Of the tough ones, those likely to endure.

FRANK O'CONNOR

for Miriam

I think of that charwoman's only child
rummaging through a box of gilded junk
in a suburban room; his captive eyes
easing into a world of surplus wealth,
the images of two worlds warring in

his head. In the darkness of an attic,
his latest images; silver-handled
brushes with engraved designs, old-smelling
bottles and elaborate dancing-cards:
a glittering code of higher living.

Later, he would fall from those heights to climb
the real hill, to walk across St Luke's
to a smaller house. Climbing those same steps,
I can imagine their cold living-room,
the last of daylight defining shafts

of dust, dust and light revolving in a
single beam. I can see his neat mother
polishing, moving chairs against a wall;
clearing the way for a night of resting:
her heart lost to a waltz of tidying.

DEATH BY FIRE

for D. H. FitzGerald

'They were very brave, really,' you say,
staring into the winter fire, 'the way
they riveted themselves to the high steel
bridge and refused to surrender.'
(By then you had taken both banks
and bullets came whistling from behind.)

One could hear a thud on the road
after a wounded sniper had fallen
from the steel grid; his blood mingled
with oil-spillage to form a dark mould.
Dying soldiers settled on the bridge-
road like flies on a window in October.

A troop of scorched butterflies falls
from the chimney-ledge, disturbed by
the fire we lit after four weeks;
during that month they had settled into
a safe winter resting place. Now
they scatter, making a bridge of smoke and
sparks from the fire to the ceiling.

One fly rises slowly; in the first sharp
leap of flame its two wings catch fire.
In the flickering light I watch it die;
it makes crippled leaps across the hob,
wings closing in, like a fish tightening
in pain, then opening again. Finally, its
wings, like a soldier's hand, relax in death.

HER BLINDNESS

In her blindness
the house became
a tapestry of touch.

The jagged end of a dresser
became a signpost
to the back-door,

bread crumbs crunching
under her feet told
her when to sweep
the kitchen floor;

the powdery touch
of dry leaves in
the flower-trough
said that geraniums
needed water.

I remember her beside
the huge December fire,
holding a heavy mug,
changing its position
on her lap; filling

the dark space
between her fingers
with the light
of bright memory.

DAEDALUS, THE MAKER

for Seán Lucy

Dactylos was silent and impersonal;
hidden behind false names, he achieved
a powerful *persona*. There was only
his work; a chipping of rock into form
and the rhythmic riveting of bronze,
diminishing his need for company.

Learning to keep silent is a difficult
task. To place Art anonymously at
the Earth's altar, then to scurry away
like a wounded animal, is the most cruel
test-piece. A proud maker, I have waited at
the temple doors for praise and argument.

Often I have abandoned an emerging form
to argue with priests and poets –
only to learn the wisdom of Dactylos:
that words make the strangest labyrinth,
with circular passages and minotaurs
lurking in the most innocent lines.

I will banish argument to work again
with bronze. Words, I have found, are
captured, not made: opinion alone is
a kind of retreat. I shall become like
Dactylos, a quiet maker; moving between
poet and priest, keeping my pride secret.

FROM
The Sorrow Garden

THE POET OF THE MOUNTAINS

Every Sunday she prepared the brown oak table
For breakfast and listened to new writers
On the wooden wireless, while she ladled
Fresh milk from the yellow stone pitchers
By the wall. The English words that broke
Across her small kitchen were seldom spoken

When she was young. Then, it was all Irish:
Those brown words had curled about her childhood
Like collies home from a long cattle-crush
Or an alphabet of trees in the Abbey wood
Where she picked bluebells with her uncle
And caught words off the air as they fell.

She had spent all her days in the company
Of women. They had churned milk in the dairy
With her, taken weak lambs across the hills,
Or spoken in black shawls as far as chapel:
All their days were taken up in a great swell
Of work. They had to wash, sew, milk and kneel.

But at night, I imagine, she would lie awake
And listen to the mountains for her own sake.
She would listen to the linen wind at night
As it flapped the wet clothes. She would steal
Into the children's room to dream and write;
To be a whole person, a picker of bluebells.

SURVIVORS OF WAR

There's a minute photograph of a troop-ship
being swallowed by the North Sea off Norway,
dying into the black light of a cold ocean;
and there's a circular intelligence shot
of Nijmegan Bridge before its capture. (That's
the special image of a war I never lived
but possess deeply on occasions.) White walls
intact, the Dutch house standing by the bridge,
is where you found the first Collected Carlos
Williams. A cluster of readable words, you took
it across the dead country on Goering's train
through the snow-landscape of defeated people,
of apologizing Burgomeisters and old gardeners,
until you gave it to me, thirty years later,
as a gift of peace, the pages fading at the edge.

THE BRIGADIER BURNING LEAVES

How many autumns? Maybe nine or ten
since we raked the first leaves
and had them stacked for burning.

This evening there was woodsmoke again,
leaving its taste on walls and eaves,
carrying the burnt year into October.

DE VALERA'S CHILDHOOD

The roots of the grandeur of the world
plunge into a childhood
GASTON BACHELARD

I

Something from his sad youth
I've been following through;
to be found, perhaps, at his
childhood Limerick village,

in the small streets, the grey
school buildings where his
copying-desk and dutiful hand-
writings are preserved. There

even his absences were seen
as duty-filled: work that gives
a clue toward understanding –
cold dutiful hours spent

before school delivering milk
to neighbours, soaking gallons
of folklore and folk-solitude
from the morning world of work.

II

Lloyd George was wary of his
fox-like comings and goings:

'all that is truly dark
and furtive and violent in

the Irish mind' was what
he thought. He should have

known that such an animal
existed only in colonial

thought. Our home fox wanted
to hunt in its own word-wood.

III

Once, in a blindness lit by memory,
De Valera recalled the penniless days
after College, herding another man's
wild cattle. A long funeral

snaked its way through the roads
below the hillside where he stood.
'Shall I end like that?', he thought,
'end all purpose within its source,

like a flower gone full cycle in
its seed, like a fox turning over
to give death with birth.' Like that
old fox he spent the final years,

staring at roads from the brushwood
of memory, retracing his steps
down wound-roads to childhood
where a broken soul could be restored.

RETURNING TO DE VALERA'S COTTAGE

Coming down the hill we could see the summer
village, mill-wheel and stream
churning up the wet sunlight.
The village seemed brighter
then without the dark weight
of his heavy cloak or a threat
of his sword-cane over their
votes. Their great child had been dead for years.

So that ordinary children came back onto the street
while adults gossiped lightly
unafraid of the official cars –
not that he was held in awe,
but the walking evidence of
so intense a life frightened
the whole village and kept them from serious thought.

In finding his cottage we found a life that was
inside ourselves. A small
moment of sorrow. A tear
riding down the glass of
our eyes like blood fall-
ing from a bullet wound.
We kicked the heap of weeds
with our heels and cursed the narrowness of the path.

Remember the summer that he died? The old English
General running across the road
wearing a black tie for his
dead adversary; making excuses,
then, for the sudden mourning
impulse – 'After all, he was old,
he was a soldier. We both pulled through our wars.'

DE VALERA, LINDBERG
AND MR COOPER'S BOOK OF POEMS

for Jane Cooper

Mr Lindberg wore his aeroplane like a tight suit, his eyes pierced
the mist, wings dipped to the sea. Mr Cooper stretched from the
dripping cockpit to watch islets and water, the intricate basketry
of landforms in the ocean. What he tried to imagine, as the air-
frame shivered, was a book of sentimental poems like a quiet
daughter on his mother's knee.

> De Valera worked in his subdued room,
> squinting echoes on the wooden floor
> shivered when his pencil rose and fell.
> Somewhere in the blind country farther
> West the dripping biplane traced an arc.
> Dev dreamed a map of the future, of the
> astonished country threaded by planes;
> cargoes landing on tarmac like the last
> consoling phrases in a civil-war poem.

After they had landed they met him in his tall room. His hands
stretched out to shake the air, his eyes never adjusting to the lack
of light. Thus he met the new Americans, the tough and techni-
cal. O *tough* they seemed, and *technical*, until Mr Cooper saw the
poems that his mother would have loved. Poems broke the
strangeness, there and then, as they roamed through the verses of
a resolved civil war. Although Mr Lindberg wore his knowledge
like a tight suit; his eyes piercing the mist, wings dipping to the sea.

IN MEMORY OF MY FATHER

Sometimes I return to where he belonged,
to his most real world of felled trees
and timber bridges;
                    and I find, where
time has had time to play,
his first dimly-lit woodlanders' hut
covered by time's macramé
of loosened ropes and beams.

Next winter when growth stiffens
I shall uncover the black derrick-beams
of his circular saw and, perhaps, the
smashed axle of an old steam truck

and (if I am really lucky) the smell
of woodsmoke from across the river
and tea brewing by the river and
him hiding his paints and sketching-pad
before calling his labourers to rest.

THE SORROW GARDEN

I   HOLE, SNOW

It is an image of irreversible loss,
This hole in my father's grave that needs
Continuous filling. Monthly now, my
Uncle comes to shovel a heap of earth
From the spare mound. Tear-filled, he
Compensates the collapse of his brother's
Frame. I arrive on my motor-bike to help
But he will not share the weight of grief.

It is six months since my father's death
And he has had to endure a deep snow;
All night it came down, silently like time,
Smoothing everything into sameness. I
Visited the winter-cold grave, expecting
A set of his footprints, a snow-miracle.

II   SMALL BIRDS, VOICES

These are the neatly twisted sounds of death,
Those small brown birds singing, small winter
Birds clinging to an overhanging bough.
Never in life did I know him to stare
So silence-stricken for one brief moment.

These birds recall the voices of his life:
A low cold note is the voice of torment
From childhood poverty and the brief, light
Notes are the tones of love and marriage.

'There's the beginning of *your* life's troubles',
A neighbour said at his grave. I arranged
The wilting wreath-flowers, feigning numbness.

Something, perhaps his voice, told me even then
How much of Love, Sorrow, Love one life contains.

III   MISTING-OVER

These bright evenings I ride
through the young plantation
by the river; at times I can
see the young trees clearly
through the collapsing mist.

Sometimes in the misted river
at dusk his face at my left
shoulder has become distinctly
settled and lined with peace.

But now in the clouded pools
I drive through on the avenue,
he no longer calls out as if
injured by my rear wheel, but
is happy as clay, roads, memory.

IV   LOST WORDS, SORROWS

It's difficult to believe that it could
go on; this wanting to participate
in a rigid plan of water and wood,
words and wood and other inanimate
worlds that cannot explain sorrow.

Around me I find the forms that know
his lack of living. The wooden sculpture
on a shelf points to its lack of finish,
calls for a finishing touch, for his sure
and solid polish. I pray for its wish.

As if water could explain my crying,
I visited the salmon-weir after
a snow-fall. The fish were manoeuvring
through the spray, determined to get over
protective obstacles of wood and stone.

Like salmon through water, like virgin wood
disturbed into its form in art, his death
obfuscates words irrecoverably. Death plays
its own tune of vision and shadow. It has
attached itself as a vocabulary of change.

HER WIDOWHOOD

Ba mhaith liom triall go deireadh lae go brónach
SEÁN O RÍORDÁIN

A shaft of wind cuts through the wet garden,
Daffodils are forced to their full shower
Of yellowness. The tall azara that smelled
Of chocolate has sprung to life once more
Though its bark was cut, its bole half sawn.
Something of the old regeneration has left
Me: birds seem quiet, the furrows less clear.
The accuracy of new growth that blessed
Love's wandering eyes at our first sowing
Seems non-existent in the huge quietness
Left by his death. Plants revolt in my head –
This widowhood is like a nettle sting,
Blotching one's whole body with its whiteness,
Filling limbs and seed with the ache of the dead.

FLOWERS FOR MY MOTHER

I

My mother has lately entered the realm
of flowers, binding with her absent man

the fresh May clay and layers of river soil
into a broad spray of local exile.

Cold they lie in these first days of summer
with time like a weed covering the scar

of memory, quietening the quick disease
into the calmer warmth of summer peace.

II

Late at night I think of their swift passing,
their quick embrace; an almost chance coupling

in the mayfly afternoons of their youth:
the casual toss in the coin of their growth

until something mutated toward the sentences
of a second son. Their light summer moods

breeze through my room now — as if those first days
had reformed, cooling all of sorrow, all of pain.

MY FATHER, READING

The wide lamps at his bedside table would burn
while he fought nervously between books and dream.
The house fell asleep before his hands reached out.

In daylight our town pursued its gossip-lines
while our father drank his tea and studied on:
his sons would come home to an absence of words
while their lives cried out to be taken in hand.

My father became famous on his word-journeys,
sailing (on extended leave) with Scott, avenging
all crime with *Four Just Men*. Every book I open
brings him to the window to strain his weak eyes
and answer our long calls with a wave of his pen.

WAKING

The world has been all roundness since we met,
a vast seashore of round thoughts, pebbles
for gathering into caskets near your bed . . .
and photographs, your world of images . . .

and a bronze circle of Chinese bells
that sail on the breeze from your window,
a circle of music that encloses your deep
thought, your deepest death –

All summer I explored your deepest death
playing with stones at the edge of your life,
touching the grainy photographs you took
that make human skin seem as cool as stone
and stones into a round inquisitive flesh.

I marvelled too long at the contours of death;
fell in love with the marvellous black colour
of grief, with the grey rain-water of sorrow
that settled into the stagnant pool of my face.

This morning the spell of it all was extinguished:
while you slept I saw death carried away from me
by the mystical gardener of the family; he carried
sorrows away like a bundle of dried mature onions.

He didn't even stop to take my courtesies, my bows,
while you slept strongly beside your herd of stone.

THEIR GOING, THEIR DYING

There's a special sorrow that we reserve
For parents, so deep that the world of love,
The world of small happenings – of babies
Born and young wives undressing for a second
Time – cannot gain access.
                                    Philosophy
Itself can hardly probe so deep. Only
The rain clouds bursting on mountains beyond
My writing window, leaves blown against glass
By the spirit of a storm, or a dog
Howling against the first frost of the year
Can reach the subjective hollow in the head.

Thus, the old impress our lives with their deaths,
Having borne us in pain to start the argument
And opened their love-filled hearts just too late
To leave us, abruptly, wondering where they went.

FLOWERS IN WINTER

Sometimes the miracle of things
that are no real miracle is

the most blessed of miracles.
Like ten minutes ago when

the Brigadier brought into
the warm kitchen a broken spray

of viburnum fragrans in full bloom
from the depths of a snow storm.

A NEUTRAL STATE, 1944

I   THE LIGHTS OF DUNLEARY

On the night journey there would be talk
of future pleasures, a subalterns' chorus
in relaxed voice about Irish chocolate cake,
real eggs and bacon and the Curragh races.

There would be the neutral yawning of the sea
above immediate memory; troubles in the black
city of war would move across their night eye
like the wash of a periscope causing an ache

of fear. But they would look across the bow
beyond the wash of sorrow, over the war-sea
to the naked lights of Ireland: (the soft glow
of De Valera's land, and her bog neutrality).

II   MACLIAMMOIR AT CAPPOQUIN

On tour he motored into the enchanted place
where dogs and cattle slept on the road, where
geese chased the actresses like jealous players
disturbed within their protected circular tour.

Between acts they floated on the tidal river,
Renaissance colours diffusing in the iridescent
pools; Coralie in her cinnamon Jewish garment
priming the water with her long, playful fingers.

That July their war-figures became broadly slow,
making Raymond say (in his eau-de-nil tights
and softened by the neutral summers of the South),
'If only the folks at the wars could see us now.'

66

A MEETING WITH PARNELL

That day's event began with a lady's parasol
tripping across the grey Victorian sands
of Dublin and two polite female calls
for help. The passing bather lent a hand.

With an athletic zest he pursued her shade,
catching it beautifully near the pebble wall
while her child and its day-nurse delayed
as their mistress practised her protocol.

'You *are* a kind man', she said, when she saw
that he was a handsome one. 'Please sit here
and take a little shade. Nobody will know:
I'm a Castle person, so you need have no fear.'

'I must warn you, Madam, about who I am,'
the dark man announced, 'I'm the awful Parnell.'
Then she feigned boredom with political games;
Things like State Affairs, she said, *make one ill.*

The sun blazed at the edge of the Century
where they spoke, and the sea came in
to wash their flirting feet. He held her baby
in his scandalous hands and it seemed

to enjoy his cheerfulness. All that afternoon
its small joy stretched across the Dublin sand,
as if it knew what foes were sharing the sun;
as if it felt a new life seeping from the land.

THE WISDOM OF AE

Some days he would wander around his attic-room
in search of a recent letter or a new poem
that might have hitched from a rural Co-op,
or an unfinished painting that had desolately
hid between newspapers and a month of bills.
His life was full of things fresh or unmade

like the new country or a spring homestead.
He kept to his own chaos in the land of hot
views; opinion like a dagger couldn't disturb
his ways or alter his deepest occult reference.
(While the land was busy with war he was perturbed
by an incomplete vision of a future President.)

Visions came and went like shafts of sunlight
at the woods near Coole; nymphs playing on the shore
were part of a permanent familiar insight;
a familiar world of rocks, woods and water.
He was the first to live by the eternal Feminine.

THE PROVINCIAL WRITER'S DIARY

On cold nights in November he read late
and worried about the gift of fiction;
he was enveloped in a shell of lethargy.
Everything was let go –
even his diary lay idle for a whole month
while he chased provincial loneliness
from the corners of his mother's house.

Everything became consumed by the Personal:
furious theatre work killed some time,
strolling with his bachelor friends, fishing,
or the steady cumulative ritual of walking
beyond the city to sketch its grey limits.
But nowhere could he find (within those limits
of thought) the zeal that would consume life.

He lived far from the heroic. On Monday
mornings he would stalk the grey ghettos
of the North side and low-lying tenements
for absentee school-children. He would be taken aback
by the oppressive stench and filth of their lives.
One morning he thought, as if explaining all misery,
that such homes were the nests of the Military.

CONVERSATION WITH AN EMIGRÉ

He is amazed by the pattern of lives.
By his own life, for instance, that
Came roaring at the door of the Ministry
With fists and expulsion orders, making
Him like a persecuted Jew from the East.

I am amazed that his wandering has
Come to such a perfect halt. His pens
Have bored deeply into American wells:
Still, the East goes wandering in his head
To irritate the peace of unfinished work
And roar at the steel door from inside.

He is startled by a riot of small birds
Stretching their muscles in November. 'Oh!
Yes!' he says when I point them out. Amazed,
He is, that even from universities birds
Still migrate southward from the storms.

THE POET IN THE CITY

to Robert Duncan

Carefully he donned his woollen cloak-coat
To brave the Pacific morning of grey
Winter quays, to mutter inside tweed folds
The names of famous foodstores in the Bay.

Heading south we were hit by an avalanche
Of Spanish tumbling from the mouths of new
Immigrant children. Then they fell into silence
While the poet and his companion passed through.

'This place was as wise as Europe before
The Mid-West was opened,' he quickens his pace,
'Those children are the latest successors:
The city's an old but democratic place.'

I watched his head turning like a nervous
Bird's or a compass-point in a mine-
Field while we scanned a shop or ducked a bus,
Searching for burritos before lunchtime.

Everywhere we turned became a maze of colour,
A mouth-watering landscape without food;
Rows of houses layered on each other,
Hundreds of flower-boxes like hanging woods.

'The multiple experience is what I'm for,'
He would say, 'Joyce and Eliot, the ample
Mystery of a city when it's bared –
And not the Helicon of country spells.'

We reached the street's end, the edge of abyss
It seemed, but behind us was his Falconress,
The city, making words soar and manoeuvre,
Guiding them to her firm, outstretched centre.

NOVEMBER IN BOSTON

for Paul and Hualing

In this place an Irishman should feel at home.
Walking from the Shamrock Restaurant into the theatre
district I cross Lismore and Waterford streets,
abundant whiskey faces, even a tricolour shyly flown
in a pub window. The cool November air
is damp and gusty, pure Atlantic, unlike the neat

interior breezes that cross the Mid-West. The older
Irish have flown by now to the warm southern places
where the sun and accents are broad and unfamiliar.
Today, people without consonants brave the Boston air;
Asian and beautiful, they Zen-ify the open spaces
where white Sweeneys had fantasized on sex and beer.

One Sunday, from a studio I looked over disused wharves
at the little Ireland. 'Snow comes down on our streets
like an extra drop of oil,' the young artist said,
'blending Asian and Irish memory into its scarf
of white.' As he spoke people fled from a hard sleet;
rich Bostonians and labourers with luncheons of bread.

Those long November evenings I was made to feel as special
as a kiwi, a small green species resurrected from
its island grave. 'Listen! He's Irish! From back there.'
It took an hour of words for expectations to dispel,
for them to find a space for one *Sweeney* gone all calm
and clean-cut, like a piece of superior export crystal.

THE PHENOMENOLOGY OF STONES

for Catherine

These summer days I carry images of stone,
Small pebbles from a photographer's shelf
Made smooth by a million years of sea and salt.
Sunlight shines roundly into their small room,
Twisting black grains into crystals and gems:
Lights call like young birds from their surfaces,
Sparrows of light flying from graves, from places
Where the dead had grown; the sorrow-gardens.

But the silence of stone quietens the mind
And calms the eye. Like their girl-collector –
In her deep solitude the stones are moved.
She is their dream-collector, pouring her kind-
ness into their sleeping form. They gather
Fables about themselves to entertain such love.

FORM

The famous photographers discuss form:
They wonder mainly about light –
Whether the form is what is, or what

Is lit. I think of your body then,
Stretching with ease, a perfect aesthetic,
Your strong loveliness an unlit weight

Waiting for another weight. I believe
That master photographer, who must have been
Lit by love, whose sacred forms were

A ship's hull moving in the water,
A polished violin at rest,
A woman's body discovering its ease.

FROM

The Non-Aligned Storyteller

IN THE LUXEMBOURG GARDENS

Nothing could be second-hand that's so full of love.
Although avenues are wrecked with tourists
In canvas shoes, afternoons full of Coke,
The dappled light of the chestnut grove
Is new, and the ludic patterns of the fountain.
The fresh dog mess on the gravel path is true
And full of words like *love, companionship, good news.*

In America, once, I heard the cicada in the trees,
A strange, continental, clicking sound, that made me feel
A total stranger. Until I recalled
The cicadas in the fields of Whitman, the cicadas
Among the empty oil-drums of Roethke. Such familial
Calls from the extensive parish of poems.

Walking with you in the Luxembourg Gardens, I heard
The childhood of many books whooping with joy;
I heard mothers giving a first-hand account of care.
I wondered which child was taking notes
For the first perfect biography of love –
We would be the passers-by in that first memory;
The Luxembourg in our talk, the chestnut light above.

WINDOWS

The windows of our flat: their shutters
disperse the worst fogs of the winter
so that I can see the quays falling
into the tidal mouth of the river –
since I moved as high as these windows
I've overheard the nightlife of ghosts:
British officers taking their boots off,
Cork whores dropping hints and slips,
their accents putting on airs. Also,
servants in the evening (the year 1901,
maybe) when all their chores were done
tip-toeing to their bedrooms. The horses
on Wellington Road are made of glass,
their liveried coachmen are throwing
wet oats at the windows of our flat.

THE MONK'S PLEASURE

from the Irish

The little bell that tinkles
in finger-strokes of wind:
that is my ecstasy
instead of a girl's hand.

MR NABOKOV'S MEMORY

For my first poem there are specific images
herded like schoolchildren into a neat row.
There is an ear and human finger hanging
from the linden tree in the Park north of
Maria Square and, between there and Morskaya
Street, other images of defeat. Such
as a black article in a Fascist newspaper
blowing along the footpath, or an old soldier
throwing insults at lovers out walking.
Even the *schveitsar* in our hallway
sharpens pencils for my father's meeting
as if sharpening the guillotine of the future.
There is only Tamara, who arrives with the poem
as something good; her wayward hair tied back
with a bow of black silk. Her neck,
in the long light of summer, is covered
with soft down like the bloom on almonds.
When winter comes I'll miss school to listen
to her minor, uvular poems, her jokes,
her snorting laughter in St Petersburg museums.
I have all this; this luxury of love; until
she says: 'a flaw has appeared in us,
it's the strain of winters in St Petersburg' –
and like a heroine from a second-rate
matinée in Nevski Street she steps into the womb
of the Metro to become a part of me forever.

So many things must happen at once in this,
this single chrysalis of memory, this poem.
While my son weeps by my side at a border
checkpoint, a caterpillar ascends
the stalk of a campanula, a butterfly comes to rest
on the leaf of a tree with an unforgettable
name; an old man sighs in an orchard
in the Crimea, an even older housekeeper

loses her mind and the keys to our kitchen.
A young servant is sharpening the blade
of the future, while my father leaps
into the path of an assassin's bullet
at a brief August lecture in Berlin.
All these things must happen at once
before the rainstorm clears, leaving one
drop of water pinned down by its own weight.
When it falls from the linden leaf I shall
run to my mother, forever waiting forever
waiting, with maternal Russian tears,
to listen to her son's one and only poem.

ANDRÉ GIDE

At La Roque the swallows called, whirling round
the house, their tight marine cries piercing air
like words cut into black marble. I remember
their broods on a fine day, the fluffy sonar sound;
and Marie standing still in a blaze of sunlight,
daisies in her hand; and her loud purr at night,
the creak of her sex life that pushed me from sleep
into the nocturnal business of the adult world.

Our Anna Shackleton was never disturbed at night
except to find the holiest way to die. Kindness
and beauty and upright posture couldn't compensate
for her poverty. I was the only male to undress
her days with care. Wanting nothing but her time,
I consumed her love like a liquorice; the two of us
lived at my herbarium, urging things to their prime.

Once, charged with Anna's love of growth, I took
a wounded starling from the grass, before the cats
shared its death. I felt that it had fallen from its
nest like an idea escaped from sentences. It shook
its mild beak and nested in my hands to pour scorn
on the idle cats. But when burdened with the earthworm
of my thought it flew back to its fields of corn.

Other starlings gathered in a warmer place. Athman
and Meriem, with their rich Mediterranean walk,
shoved spices in my face. Meriem dropped her *haik*
at the door one night to cure my tubercular limbs
with a firm and mellow skin. But Athman I remember
best, weeping as my train left the oasis. Through him
the desert wept to see me going North to thought.

TO CARVE A RED TULIP

I. M. SEAMUS MURPHY

The little apprentice with a year of Art School
Under his arm, he tip-toed nervously
Between stones, the tea and biscuits of ridicule,

The suspicious lives of artisans standing on edge –
Until they gave him a tulip to carve in stone,
And stone fell to his eye like words off a page.

HOURS AGO, 1973

for D.H.F.

It's two hours since you went to the river
In the green Anglia with uncle Walter's satchel.
You forgot the box of flies on the dresser
Wrapped in a sheet of greaseproof paper.
The flies you took will serve you just as well,
You hunt for things with such exquisite care.

There's been dust at the cross-roads for weeks
With the heat, brilliant sunlight on the trees,
Every day of your annual leave. Pheasants leap
Into the tall grasses, wild animals hiss
And turn at play. So far from Ebury Street,
You've been hunting and saving their brightness

For a London winter. The warmed-up house
Is waiting for you with its brand new face.
Thirsty birds peck at the window, a vase
Of fresh foliage has been set in place.
Your soup has been left to simmer
For over two hours now. For nearly ten years.

PARTICULARS

Tonight I think about your flat in Sundays Well;
the window where you worked at stories,
the high window where rainstorms whistled.
I wonder if that house was really haunted
by a ghost that wandered from the dripping hall?
Your little room was a store house of virtue,
simple blessings peeled from its walls.
I could see them peeling when you were happy,
humming the brown tunes of Randy Newman
or spreading pineapples on a grilled gammon.

I wish I could remake that most particular time –
the delayed action of toilet soap
when you breezed past after an evening shower,
your body wrapped in a black Malayan robe;
or your critical eyes in front of a picture,
knowing it had missed what you were after.
How can I recall all that new love had noted:
the shape of boxes, the roundness of shells, the firm
and lovely amber of your breasts. The rains
that touched your glass intrude now on my writing-desk.

THE PRESIDENT'S MEN

There's dust on Mr Dineen's boots! Where has
he been canvassing, I wonder? What house
has unlatched a half-day of harvest work
to listen to his talk? My father knows
the Party poll, the roll-calls of promise;
the roads we shall take when I am older
in search of power. We'll find it like cress
on farms of green and vegetal water.

The sound of bagpipe music! Just listen!
From my father's shoulder I can see above
the crowd, Mr Dineen's careful parade,
men struggling to keep the roadway open,
sunlight in my father's hair, the glitter of
pipers' braids; the President's cavalcade.

QUESTION TIME

Question time at the end of another Election Year;
Senators and their wives dancing on the ballroom floor;
children in corners dropping crisps and cream,
their fathers ordering them home, their mothers in crimplene
having to put them outside to sulk in the Christmas dark.
Enmities dissolving now in a sea of drink and smoke and talk.

Who was Robert Emmet's mistress? Who was Kitty O'Shea?
Which IRA man was shot on his own wedding-day?
How many death-warrants did Kevin O'Higgins sign?
So much to answer between the buffet meal and wine –
But the prize is a week in Brussels, money for two,
and kisses from two Euro-MPs just passing through.

THE NON-ALIGNED STORYTELLER

Soon there would be no reason to remember Parkers
in that place. Because the present prevails . . .
PATRICK WHITE: *The Tree of Man*

Everything that happened here, that could be trapped
By light, lies abandoned in my shop:
Who would bother to look, now that my lease
Is up? I have photographic plates
Of weddings as old as any villager's memory;
A perfect plate of the first Model T in town,
A file of annual Blackwater floods, action shots
From the Carnival held for the Abbey chapel –
All of them useless. I gave my only child
A box of unclaimed, unknown Communion
Prints, perfectly justified and guillotined;
So perfect, in fact, that the subjects couldn't pay.
The first thing I photographed in this town
Was fire, a subject dangerous and ephemeral
Brought on by politics. The new Party
Had made its first great leap. That time,
The poor in celebration burned tar in barrels.
Fire made a kaleidoscope of wet streets.

I loved to stroll about in windy rain to watch
Streets training themselves to be abandoned.
By then the young had begun to disappear,
Leaving a melancholia like a dark pothole
That only the rains could fill. In the long
Afternoons of Sundays there would be a flood
Of black shawls and a brief sleet of children
As well as a drought of able-bodied men –
Factories overseas had claimed them, or a combination
Of TB and the ever-promising vagrant sea.
The villagers never trusted me, so for years
I photographed only what they could trust and see:

Corpus Christi processions, sycamore trees, local
Football teams or scullers bolting down the river.
But politics was the most awkward field. I hung
Around to collect images at the centre of its
World; dragging old men from the stifling alcoves
Of meetings. I didn't know what I was meant to see

Because I was called in at the end of events
With camera and tripod. My wife arranged
The lights above their heads. She created
An aura of strength around their tired faces,
A sort of grey metallic, a solder of wisdom.
Their chairman I remember best. He wore
A gold watch-chain to every meeting;
He had a voice as revered as a Miraculous Medal –
That gold chain sparkled in my best photographs,
Though I tried to dampen it in the negative.
His secretary owned innumerable fields.
I photographed him in one perfect moment
During a 1960 snowstorm; a starched
Figure caught against a herd of yearlings.
My wife remembers them too, under our lights,
As they held resolutely to tenancies and laws.
'If only they had strength,' she used to say, when
They were building anew, shedding bloody days.

THE EXPELLED DEPUTY

I see you once again in the flickering ballroom
of my childhood. You celebrate as usual
by dancing with so many Party women.
You held your quota as firmly as a female waist.
They all knew about your sexual barn-dance games.

They were happy conspirators, waltzing between
chairs and husbands. In the late Sixties there was no end
to your charm. A brand new Ford Zephyr
blocked the ballroom entrance. It was a chancer,
like you, taking chances by moonlight.

I watch you now in the post-Election furore.
You are gross, even more vulgar and without friends
in the new Dáil. Your name is already off certain lists.
Can you survive among the emptier projects of life?
The media nibble at you briefly. They have other projects,
but you had the best tallymen. You had their wives.

SHOPKEEPERS AT THE PARTY MEETING

Listen! Listen to shopkeepers talking
about the problems of land,
the breaking up of an estate
or a new acquisition.
Their conversation is
proprietorial. To talk
about a landlord's problem,
to articulate his burden,
is their act of possession.
They are owning the landscape,
briefly, with the magical
deeds of speech.

The Minister on the other hand
has no such words.
Whatever he has is secret,
even his desires. Especially his desires.
Shopkeepers move around the room, excited, in debt,
spilling their dreams like salt.

PARTY SHRINE

Come back,
Poor Twenty-Sixer. Live on lack.

AUSTIN CLARKE

My father is clearing the first Party shrine:
it is the summer of Sixty-Six.
He hates physical work and everything
that keeps him from the protection racket
of crosswords and history books.
But the rest of the Committee
has been drunk since the Jubilee
and can't break the spell of itself.

Weeds know nothing about the Party
or how it emerged, genie-like,
out of an abandoned shell case.
The weeds and their friends the shitting
pigeons want to bury this shrine
in a single summer.
I am holding the shovel for my father
while he reads inscriptions on brass:
sixteen golden names of the Party,
the twenty-six grammatical flaws.

THE TALKER

Silence attended his funeral after all.
After all that fuss,
the air is an immense and empty wave
as indifferent and light as old news.

They said that he talked to newspapers,
flooded the constituency with private details
while the Party wept.
He did not! But the secrets

that he filed in his heart,
the sweet and remembered, the bitter
and contemporary,
are sealed for good in his impartial grave.

THE HEALTH MINISTER

Some who held Ministries were honest, even holy.
The Health Minister, for instance, with his minuscule voice;
as if poverty had taken his breath away.
His hands stretched over the tenements of the ugly,
the poor and tubercular.
His plans tore through the landscape of suffering
to deposit clinics, hospitals; the balsam of care.

THE CHAIRMAN'S WIDOW

The Secretary moves around the room, checking.
Whose membership cards are out of date, whose cousins
have just arrived to pack the Party meeting;
who hasn't made a change of district known?
To cheat is a common enough ambition,
as natural in the countryside as sexual sin.

As the only woman here I should know
what menfolk leave behind: their feelings of love
and fair play wave goodbye at every window.
Even caution weakens when they drive away,
making every vote inevitable and hard;
as learned by rote as numbers on a Party card.

Who now remembers the timid gait of my husband,
his damaged leg? Every polling day of his life,
the way he checked and schooled the most stupid.
How pain gave him a precise and concrete mind?
The way he found strength was a joy
to the Party. His integrity was a godsend.

God send them something new, better than all of this;
this double-checking male world of myth
that coagulates into a steel and vengeful thought
to cripple love. I each them more than Party life
or else politics will be an endless, wordy game;
whole futures dying in its bleak, marcescent frame.

TO A POLITICAL LEADER

after Faiz Ahmed Faiz

Hands tied year after year with circumstances,
gone astray in the black bosom of compromise;
thoughts helpless as plankton against the sea
or butterflies strafing the immense hillsides –

Until the whole becomes darkness. Immense
night. Too many wounds in policy for the eyes
to accept. Action has become a dense
web, a protective network of cowardice . . .

That the dawn may bring immense butterflies!

TOAST

No lovelier city than all of this,
Cork city, your early morning kiss;
peeled oranges and white porcelain,
midsummer Sunday mists
that scatter before breakfast.

Mass bells are pealing in every district,
in the Latin quarter of St Luke's,
the butter *quartier* of Blackpool.
Each brass appeal calls to prayer
our scattered books and utensils,

the newly blessed who've put on clothes.
Why have I been as lucky as this?
to have found one so meticulous
in love, so diffident yet close
that the house is charged with kinetic peace.

Like a secret lover, I should bring
you bowls of fresh roses, knowing
that you would show them how to thrive.
Lucky it's Sunday, or I'd have
to raid the meter for spare shillings!

Or, maybe I should wash my filthy socks,
fret at the curtains, iron clothes,
like you after Sunday breakfast.
Normal things run deep, God knows,
like love in flat-land, eggs on toast.

LOVE'S WAR

I CARDINALS, HOSTILITIES

A coldness between us for hours; if this
goes on our love will freeze,
days will go silent and sing nothing.
Small birds, my love, have no jury to coax them
back to life. Sparrows rise and fall
without the aid of law. When pheasants die
their chicks take off alone, without aid –
neither have they Cardinals to say
a Mass for peace, to sue God for grace;
to shake blessings at their hostile fleets.

II BIRD-SONG, BELL-SOUND

Then again, let us clear our heads of sorrow:
life calls freely, bird-song, bell-sound;
the ousel and blackbird all sing. The wind
in the trees, it sings. The sea, even it makes
a tranquil tide. Now the evening makes free
with peace. When you wear bright blue
the air comes back to summer. Its light is wholesome.
And again, whole days are full of sexual music,
immensities. Your words fill the air with love.

THE DARK

You've spent the last few days
apart from me, chemically apart,
wandering from tray to tray.
Your hair has been tied back
like a Victorian woman's
bending under a reading lamp.
When I get a glimpse I see
your whole face screwed up
as if your eyes had come upon
a serious fictional event.

Can we talk? Can we talk?
Not now you whisper —
you are a nurse giving me
the correct visiting hours;
your chemical patients are
at their critical temperature.
The safety-light
is all you can go by
to see new portraits forming
in the agitated tray.

CÔTE D'AZUR

Terra firma was soon out of sight
that Friday in July. At your side,
later, my ears ached when the plane
lost height and developed weight.
Hostesses were dumb with disdain
when I refused the things you ate:

not to mention the Mid-Europeans
in the *wagon-lit*, pained
with anger at our all-night
loving noise. We turned out
at Nice to be stoned by light
and the male heat of the South.

There, long promenades were ablaze
with sunlight. For seven days
and nights we fried our marriage
near the sea, while strolling
between bright ice-cream carriages
and a tap-dancer in his ring

of Twenties music. He seemed at home
in his cool and muscular cotton;
like you in your confident
nudity. You took to the water
like the ship to Corsica, in a scent
of salt water and Ambre Solaire.

My creamed and sun-burned love,
with the little training you have
you dared to go out much farther
where waves were as hard as shingle;
leaving you very nearly scared
and your husband very nearly single.

COMBING YOUR HAIR

At first you combed your hair by the mirror
With your back to me, the sunlight
Catching the henna where it strayed.
It was a private meeting you were having there.

Then I cut my hair to your liking. We talked.
About my hair for instance, the way
It's always weak and very thin
Like tea-bag tea too early in the morning.

Now you comb your hair while I look,
While I direct your combing here and there
Toward the straight and perfect partings
Where henna waits in ambush for us both.

FROM

Seven Winters in Paris

A BOWL OF PEAS

for Catherine

A bowl of freshly depodded peas
is overturned and peas go peppering across the floor,
rat-a-tat, rat-a-tat. The dog follows,
sniffing, and flexing his pliable left ear.

One pea escapes from the impressionist sunlight.
A basket on the window is filled with
freshly picked courgettes and tomatoes,
their colour making a polyptych of stained glass.

There is a smell of woodsmoke. It is autumn
again at Glenshelane, in 1975 or '76.
Our shirts are stained with sweat, our hands grown numb
from the breaking of bonfire wood, the antics

of our old Allen scythe. Our adolescent
moments drop from the wheel of sunlight
like a potter's large vase awaiting fulfilment.
Clay is full of love. There is a blob of light

from the future, like a cuckoo-spit on wild grass.
My whole life was preparing itself for you then.
Your parallel life was like a camera made to pass
over me, tracking roundly, taking it all in.

SEVEN WINTERS IN PARIS

> *But the girl I was in love with was in Paris then,*
> *and I did not take the first train, or the second*
> *or the third.*
>
> HEMINGWAY: *A Moveable Feast*

I

Vuillard's hospitable and gifted portraits:
their eyes, passport-lens,
wandering from Conté to Conté.

II

There was no Thomas MacGreevy waiting
with a stroke of orange in his morning-dress,
but undiplomatic Paris:
fireflies on the rosewood spinet.

III

The bicycles go by in trees and trees
through the dusk of the Invalides.
Raising love-dust, bicycles become leaves –
Marguerite Yourcenar is dead.

IV

Two referenda lost, we took the inner seats
and flew to Paris through wind and sleet.

V

Should we go now, to spread the gospel
of poems, ten Métro tickets surviving
in your purse. For Garret Parnell is dead.

VI

To embrace you, like the Orly security-man:
ah! Irlandais! Your body
is the accent I uncover and uncover.

VII

I am in the Métro beside you thinking
of you faraway in the Métro –
for you have slipped away into a paperback.

VIII

You standing in front of the grey fresco
of Picasso's workshop –
wearing the talisman of a barely pink
scarf, red rag to a bull.

IX

Post-war Elizabeth had just escaped her *Seven Winters*
to fall in love again in Paris.
O Charles Ritchie! Theirs was the high love of mandarins;
the Peace Conference a mere split infinitive.

X

Seven winters in love in Montmartre,
continental snow in the attic glass –
it would be cold cold cold, but dry
enough to keep the Dáil out of our hearts.

XI

Even Beckett left behind the malaise
of ourselves by switching tongues.
Love, we withdraw from the mess of the Dáil
by flying Aer Lingus to Charles de Gaulle.

XII

The overflowing eyes of Notre-Dame-de-Lorette:
night has been milking the apartments,
loins are feeding in the ninth arrondissement.

XII

Your soul, when I touch it precisely,
lights up
like the sudden tint of auburn hair.

XIV

I'll be a Sartre to your Simone,
a damaged I, perplexed libido.
But let this be plain:
Paris is a Camus-type, *the wan bliss on the rim.*

XV

Hausmann's boulevards before our eyes,
crown jewels of the radiant Republic.

XVI

Holistically speaking, to love you
is no more difficult than this:
daylight and skylines
in your eyes. Eyes that have this
are always endless.

XVII

Though you are always the best place to write in,
better even than Paris with the forbidding rain,
without back-pain or kidney-pain or heart-pain.

XVIII

While you dress above the shutters and cobbles
the morning sun comes to wash the open pages,
pregnant with leaves – as pregnant
as Ezra Pound in Paris.

XIX

You have rushed before me into daylight
leaving a trail of human leaves –
the light in your hair
would make any Conradh lose its *craobh*.

XX

Let me kiss you on the Balard Line;
we need not take the first or second train.

XXI

And Montmartre will be taken down
and used in evidence.
While the Party fell apart
we wasted centimes at the café of *poésie*.

Conradh: League   *craobh*: branch

XXII

The Luxembourg Gardens. A school of chairs
sitting empty, awaiting *Herald Tribune* or *Le Monde*.
A busker makes a hundred notes on solitude.

XXIII

Dead for France, dead for Liberation –
a pock-mark, two pock-marks, near
St Germain-des-Prés:
the splintered cheek-bones of Christ.

XXIV

The Latin Quarter. You are my Héloïse;
only time will tell if I lose my marbles.

XXV

The bicycles speed past Picasso's studio:
horses on their way, pedalling, to see
the thoroughbreds of M. Delacroix.

XXVI

I beat a retreat from St.-John Perse;
his first editions beyond our reach –
sycamore leaves litter the shop-front
like tunic fragments at Austerlitz.

XXVII

Here's the ghost of Ezra Pound,
maestro, tulip-eater,
lost in Arthur Waley and never found.

XXVIII

In the Ile de la Cité we meet Denis Devlin,
a polite ghost, remember?
'I hear the poets have lost their marbles,
and the Dáil has burned Parnell's heart.'

'Yes, sir. And they were supposed to eat it.'

XXIX

The fever of travel is upon our marriage;
the world is all French when we toss and turn.
Our nerves are alive with it –
Perrier shivers in the tooth-glass.

XXX

The overhead drone in the shallow Métro.
All the haunted traffic of the Gare du Nord;
1848, the first tricolour, Stephens
and Stephen D. 'Parysis, *tu sais*, crucycrooks',
sweet, the honeycomb of exile.

THE GATHERING OF WAVES

The waves gather differently off the coast of Crete;
they are less demented by the inland sea,
though kicked by wind from the Turkish coast.
The sea is grey there, Ottoman, moody.
At Agio Roumeli in the deep south
the shore is red-hot, the sea aquamarine,
plankton-less, like a melting mirror.
The waves are more generous, rhythmic, natal,
like a mould made specially for naked breasts.

You are always heading for the ocean,
unhappy until you can eavesdrop on water
and the waves' conversations.
The sea must be an adequate listener
or an expansive, avuncular teller of tales.
Happy with your feet in water,
you are always calling to me at the shore,
telling me what the sea is,
what a lover can't miss, what the ocean tells you.

Not to understand this is to be a mariner
beached, or a convict on an island
watching the waves gather, listening,
waiting for the one chance to be gathered in.
It is four years, Catherine,
four years that disappear in the sea's mirror.
I see you most clearly then by the ocean,
at Agio Roumeli, you calling me, excited,
wanting to share the salt-water's potable memory.

EDOUARD VUILLARD

1868–1940

Your mother at the window knitting, green drapes;
and outside the soft yellow-stone of Paris;
or your mother watering hyacinths, the floral
tablecloth, reluctant light falling upon her face.
Or your mother at the table, writing,
a cup and newspaper, an ormolu mantle-clock,
or your mother preparing dinner at the rue de Calais.
You painted her through the plethora of cushions:
for your subject was your mother,
the miraculous painter of the household;
the miraculous, trapped, underestimated mother.
What luck you had, Edouard Vuillard,
to know so deeply a trapped untroubled mother,
to leave so beautifully the filial evidence.

Few poets, perhaps Boris Pasternak,
were lucky like this –
and it made of him a huge untoppled romantic:
art, art, art, untoppled romantic.
For who can deny life? Who can deny it
when a child stirs in the womb
like a fine brush stirring on the palette,
when a mother knits finely by lamplight.
For you were never orphaned like us, Party-less,
as orphaned as I felt in the Musée d'Orsay;
orphaned as winter trees in La Place Vintimille.
Your mother at the window, knitting, her green drapes:
one can turn love inside out without loss of style.

ELLEN TOBIN McCARTHY

*

You were as psychic as my father
was confused. Nowadays I am haunted
by you and the menagerie of ghosts –
they are wings of loneliness.

*

Life was a mystery to you –
domestic life was a form of magic:
you always watched the ring of a cooker
as if it was the aurora borealis.

*

A gun behind the picture of The Sacred Heart;
the fear of uniforms. Your half-brother
lost a foot in some Monaghan skirmish –
our poor Republic! The poor always cop it.

*

Why should I love this dead town?
You were humiliated unto death.
The Rich wouldn't touch us with a ten-foot
pole, or even a number nine iron.

*

In moments of weakness when I believe in God
instead of the anarchist ideologue, Christ,
I recall the frightening of women by priests,
their Maria Corelli faces, their pitiful beads.

*

You are sitting in my father's lap;
it is a cold day in late October –
you rediscovered each other near the end,
but not before you broke our hearts.

*

I watch the minutes passing away:
the minutes are like bark of *olearia*
blowing along the grass after a storm:
each bark a negative of your dead face.

*

There is a fire burning in the bedroom
the night before my First Communion.
You re-enter, again and again,
to absorb the anointed firelight.

*

To be lucky in love is the best thing,
you insisted. Better than all the wealth
in Dungarvan. Which is why
you switched fiancés at seventeen.

*

I must have seen you crying often
after a Friday morning deluge of bills;
but it is your girl's infectious laugh
that reaches here through the years.

*

Leaves blown against the gutter,
bloodied leaves of Virginia creeper;
an untrained growth is void of conversation,
sterile as an unexamined life.

*

The Dáil assembles for a new session;
there's a Deputy still in prison.
How quickly you would have lit candles
for Gregory, as you did for Noel Browne.

*

Suffering anointed you for death.
You were adored at seventeen;
at thirty-seven you had the weight of love –
you were Mary without Elizabeth.

*

I visit your grave for the first time,
Nel, mother. The hardened earth
brings countless humiliations to mind –
no mystical blackbirds, no sparrows.

MERCY HOSPITAL

for David Kiely

I   RECOVERY ROOM

Dear kidney, now you know it all,
all the folly of a fight
for one sober poet's life –
this feverish April dawn
I watch the gifted nurses,
the ones with Nastassia Kinski eyes,
I watch them inspecting sutures,
replacing drip-feeds, dispensing pethidine.
Their bird-like coming and going,
their trans-wall St Martin de Pores quality
has made me realize
how much I need this life.
Any other Paradise
would be a second-rate surprise.

II   FEVER

A tall house-officer with long black hair
and a Montenotte accent, but lovely still
with the solace of all that knowledge,
takes a thermometer and sighs.
My room is sick with heat, and sick
with the kindness of so many flowers;
their pungent agricultural *adieu*.

III   SACRED HEART

I know I've lost weight already,
suspended from the mean
umbilical of an intravenous drip.
But this is the end of the pain-twilight.

My soul has better hearing,
the body is clairvoyant, soaring
with the loss of pain. The picture
of the Sacred Heart on the wall
has watched over me. It hasn't moved:
you can report this to my cousins,
it hasn't moved from its Italianate
open-heart surgery. You move, though,
from hope to window to hope,
reciting your effective opuscules –
Don't worry
this is not a dry run for a funeral.
And smile. You are the healing Magdalen.

IV   VENETIAN LIGHT

My eyes blink and moisten, waking
in the Venetian light
of the first oliguric hours.
There are spots of sunlight on the wall,
disintegrating emboli of dawn.
My body has become the template
of renewal, a more pliable friend.
Much better, thank you. The suffering
Christ on the wall is more distressed-
looking than me, thank God.
Diffuse light that has stirred me
from the multiple nerve-block
of surgery is nothing less
than a consecrated bell
struck by the nescient sister in the corridor.
Pethidine is working still. It clears
the corridors for the Sanctus bell.

To be worried about a friend's poems,
to be restored to a need for friendship,
is the greatest blood-count in the world.
My body is easing away from pain,
it has escaped the cut flowers:
Thank you very much.
I have escaped the haunted hospice.
On my bedside table are Seferis's poems,
the shipwreck of his days in pain.
'It is easier,' he wrote,
'to interview a Cabinet Minister
than to book a surgeon's knife.'
His prayers are on my table now,
sun-drenched, even existentializing
Christ's Passion. *Who knows?*
Going down the neon corridors
of anaesthesia there is nothing, nothing
like 'Mathios Paskalis Among the Roses'.

BEES IN THE RAFTERS

Here I struggle to make a stern diary of love,
Moved by the intimate guest in your womb.

There is a flutter at the centre
Of the sexual paradiso. *Have you felt life?*

Like a mouse stirring among the sheaves
Or rogue honey-bees in the rafters.

But it is something wholly good, the psychic gift
And, also, more like a movement in the heart.

Even the trees are attempting an essay on love
With their red quality-ink of October.

There is a gathering in of everything in
Julie's place because of the rampant summer.

Late bees, drunk with the falling temperature,
Carry their late resources to where we are.

It is easier to speak of death than love;
We're better at idolizing politics than sex.

But I wish to frame the autumn of one mother-to-be,
To make autumnal your summer-loving fertility.

There is a movement at the centre of our days,
Just as the long hot summer moved the country.

Cathy, rogue bees in the rafters, October stores,
Embody the new meaning of what was only words.

LISTENING TO KATE INEZ

I

You frightened the life out of us,
Kate Inez. Bored with growth,
you fell asleep in the womb
or took to reading in the dark.

Little boats out of Helvick,
carrying arms or armless,
never moved as quietly through fluid.
Worried by your silenced voice

we sought the voice that was you,
the fetal heart-beat on a monitor.
The gifted radiographer – all heart,
earth-mother – made you whole.
It was our happy coming-of-age.
We took the afternoon off,
champagned that brief encounter
bathed in the light of ultrasound.

II

Boats creaked along the Libyan Sea
in the month you were conceived.
Our caïque fled the lukewarm food
that was served at Agio Roumeli.

Only the stones were hot,
red-hot with the heat of Cretan sun
and the military jets that blazed
overhead, leaving their sinister trails.

The sea was quiet at Loutron
when the boat cut its engines
and came to rest. Your new mother moved
to the light-drenched bow

to photograph the phosphorescent wharf
while you held on to amoebic life.
Soon this would be a dark sea, with dead
baby Stylianopoulou, dead Hana Gadafy.

III

But you survived it all!
I hear your laughter in the next room.
It's your mother's tickling skill
teasing the graduate of her womb.

She's so skilled at this; an artist,
she could tickle Satan and make
him good. The way she tickled
your father with her artistic limbs
to become a conceiver in the sun,
the way she turned to love, a seal
in the love-ocean. All her good
qualities can become an organic

node of tickling. Your laughter, Kate,
is what you've taken from us both.
But the other thing, the Libyan Sea,
is the unique node of your destiny.

A DAUGHTER'S CRY

At four in the morning we are stirred
by her small insistent night-cry,
like the *ping ping* of a digital clock
in the night air. Her mother
runs before me to staunch the wound
(the night is bleeding strong tears,
the moist cradle is calling for love).
Kate Inez, Kate Inez. Her mother's
weary arms are as strong as motherhood
and coiled against the moonlight,
its natural fawn-like trembling.

When she was born the birds sang
a dawn chorus on Old Blackrock Road.
Nothing stirred but blackbirds
that opened their souls like eyelids,
while we called her name, her name,
across the new, victorious daylight.

A JULY AFTERNOON ON JAMESON'S FARM

The scents of summer at Tourin,
dappled light on fruit trees.
The farm manager is full of praise
when we strip the bushes clean.
His dog is barking near the jeep
parked at the weighing-shed,
its long tongue a brilliant red
like the skin of July berries.
We are the small *bearachs* in
this life who come to earn their keep
with little hands and plastic cups,
who chafe their white Catholic skins
and mutter insults at each bush
that unleashes a clump of nettles.
One midday we'd already settled
into work when a Southern cloudburst
finished us. For nearly two hours
we sat and played. Our pants were wet
from the leaves deflecting sleet.
Adults went off to the woodstore
for comfort, some lithe teenage girls
coaxed shelter from the tractor lads.
Others went back to Cappoquin
expecting more south-western squalls.

Each July we'd wait for rain to clear,
half-dazed in the moist atmosphere,
until the daughter of the house
raced out with the manager's labrador
to stir workers back to the farm.
Her thick hair was blonde as the sun,
her voice like some homeopathic film
to ease our hail and nettle scars.
Once I was so amazed by her good looks
that I fell headlong into a fruit-box,

covering my face with brilliant juice;
my embarrassment as strong as hate –
her eyes Elizabethan blue, amused.

SUMMER RAIN IN BALLYFERRITER

More flashy July knapsacks gather at Ballyferriter,
church and supermarket remain open
to collect whatever pollen of summer business
is still unsettled. Sybil Point
rises and falls among the sisterly hills of mist;
night bobbing like a fishing float,
our minds bobbing, bookless, without ballast.
Our child stirs in her cot. She moves constantly
in her *naomhóg* of sleep while the wind
finds a crevice for its fingers. Windows rattle
and sigh with the strength of young seals.

Dusk falls with the stealth of illegal immigrants:
hundreds of Kerrymen, land-seals of Ballyferriter.
Two have already come home from Boston,
air-coffined home as luck would have it.
Luck like the language is overrun.

Incessant rain still, the thunderous colander
of the sea, a deepening of the *droth-shaol*;
this, and the waffling jurisdiction of the Dáil.
Words and their sister, the sea wind,
batter the late nocturnal bog-iris.
Knapsacks flash in the rain, youths disappear in oils.

naomhóg: Kerry term for a boat made of wood and skin
droth-shaol: an expression used by old country people to describe
  the hard life of the past

THE EMIGRATION TRAINS, 1943

A pound-note was the best kind of passport
In those days, so I held my pound tight
After my mother turned away. Idlers
Waved farewell from Ferrybank corners.
There was nothing heroic about my going,
Nothing like a political destiny –
I'd just wasted a summer standing round
Until a job came up on the Underground.

I felt destitute, like a vagrant, until
At Waterford station I realized
My good luck: I owned a suitcase of card
While others carried mere bundles of cloth.
At Kilkenny every carriage was filled
To the door. One mother's last grip held fast
Despite the moving train, the rising glass.
For some it was the last touch of a child.

There was nothing pathetic about this:
Look at the Jews, their brave, brave faces –
At least we had our own State to leave from.
Now the emigrant ship was like a big town;
That night it was Clonmel or Cappoquin
With bars open and arguments outdoors,
Politics racing through bleak corridors.
We are heading for England and the world
At war. Neutrality we couldn't afford.
I thought I would spend two years away
But in the end the two became twenty.
Within hours we'd reach the junction at Crewe
And sample powdered eggs from the menu
As well as heavy bombs falling nearby;
All that fatal traffic of an alien sky.

I was so raw and Irish at the time
They said that shamrocks grew out of my ears.
I wasn't alone with my homesick mind:
When we sailed into Holyhead our tears
Made one bitter tide. One labourer's voice
Rose out of the ship like a skylark's,
Singing *Kevin Barry, Kevin Barry.*
His song became our night-cry at the dock.

THE STANDING TRAINS

> *. . . and I thought how wonderful to miss*
> *one's connections; soon I shall miss them*
> *all the time.*
>   LOUIS MACNEICE: *The Strings Are False*

From the windows of a standing train
you can judge the artwork of our poor Republic.
The prominent ruins that make Limerick Junction
seem like Dresden in 1945
and the beaten-up coaches at Mallow Station,
the rusted side-tracks at Charleville,
have taken years of independent thought.
It takes decades to destroy a system
of stations. On the other hand, a few
well-placed hand-signals can destroy a whole
mode of life, a network of happiness.
This is our own Republic! O Memory,
O Patria, the shame of silenced junctions.
Time knew we'd rip the rails apart, we'd sell
emigrant tickets even while stripping
the ticket-office bare. The standing trains
of the future were backed against a wall.

Two hens peck seed from the bright platform,
hens roost in the signal-box.
Bilingual signs that caused a debate in the Senate
have been unbolted and used as gates:
it's late summer now in this dead station.
When I was twelve they unbolted the rails.
Now there's only the ghost of my father,
standing by the parcel-shed with his ghostly
suitcase. When he sees me walking towards him
he becomes upset. *Don't stop here!* he cries.
Keep going, keep going! This place is dead.

SAN CLEMENTE STATION, 1978

for Bill Roth

The train steams south towards summer
on this mediocre January day,
dull and soft like a Waterford holiday.
Early mist and thin newspapers
make a simple breakfast fare:
news-stands are light with the post-coital
triste of Christmas in the Carter era.
There is a ceiling on public pay
and local fires in Santa Ana,
though mist may spread to save the day.

We have been travelling this Amtrak line,
a beautiful Hispanic girl and I
and two navel cadets from Oregon.
We've slipped through the suburbs of LA,
the back-lots of a million homes,
to exchange used papers, sections
of the *Los Angeles Times*; and complain
about the price of records, rail-tickets,
real estate in the Santa Ana hills.
We lose the suburbs as abruptly
as the mist that clears. The sea, Oceanside,
palm trees, then orange groves appear
like colour slides flung at the train.
At San Clemente Station the waves
murmur across the embankment: water
absorbs a picture of itself pulling in.

Well, I'm home. Our girl companion
gathers her January shopping bags
and turns to go. A bronze surfer
catches her eye through the window
and they smile. I think
of their renewed Pacific sex life.
'You must be happy to be home.'
No. No
I hate coming back to San Clemente,
my mother's on her own, depressed.
While oceanic sunlight floods the train
I think of my father's sudden death.
It's eighteen months now, he died in June.
This is the farthest I've ever been from home.

335.04

Dampness has eaten away at the *Dunferry Risin*.
Ninety years have waterlogged the author's name:
Moran is missing, only *J. J.* survives
in the grey fog of the spine –
the author as his mother knew him
or as the IRB might have known him
in the familial secretive world.
It was praised by an MP in *The Evening Sun*,
generous in Victorian London's neutrality.
This is the best picture ever of the IRB.

398.21

Lennox, should we move you from fiction to 398?
For years you haven't moved from the fiction shelf;
your *A Young Man from the South* is brown with rot,
should we throw it out? The folklore
that coloured your pen was overwhelming
and overwhelmed so many with love –
love of country is such a blessed thing,
Fay's Abbey Theatre, Yeats' *Kathleen Ni Houlihan*.
We've moved from Willie to Enoch Powell,
from the soft porn of Lennox consumed
to the steel horn, hard as Wolverhampton nails.
Lennox, welcome to the sceptical librarian
who hauls you out of time, fiction and pain.

941.591

Rain seeps through the hoarding on the broken window;
Corkery rain, insistent, dramatic.
Youths are playing darts against the library
door, challenging me to respond:

public servant, hated. Bull's eye!
Tina, these two are gone mouldy, will I
throw them out? A note from Sheila
attached to *The Whiteboys* by Mrs S. C. Hall
and D. M. Lenihan's *The Red Spy* –
the red spy a Dublin Castle agent
forever on the threshold of quiet, of death.

364.

This is what fiction can do to a country:
a battle-cruiser in the Gulf, destroyers off Blackpool
for the Conservative conference. Who will
unwind the paranoia? The poets? The courts,
God help us. There is the question of the Birmingham Six,
Diplock Courts, the literally bloody mess
left by a murdered machine, botched revolution.
Too many brushes with the wrong tribunal –
I commit Canon Sheehan
to the library trash-can,
seven pages missing from his *Glenanaar*
as pages have fallen away from the statute books
to expose the raw powers of the State.
Too late to save *Glenanaar*, its conspirators,
the late Canon's quality of remembrance.
This is what terror can do to a novelist.

920.

George Bartram, this can't be your life-story;
Fisher Unwin's *White-Headed Boy*
that has languished in the biography section
for twenty years, another Irish tale
to satiate the post-Pre-Raphaelites.
Bertram, who are your children's children?
Did you know the Sinn Fein candidate,
Louis Walsh – the South Derry hopeful?
– Louis has drawn a pen-portrait of '48,

The Next Time, with O'Connell, Duffy, Davis.
The whole of our lives, a hundred years
of biography masquerading as novels
and novelists moonlighting as MPs.
Ours was an abrupt and botched revolution;
coitus interruptus, impermanent as binding-wax.

327.415

Power after absolution, chimeric prestige,
prison is the perfect background for an MP
When We Were Boys is what William O Brien
made of two years inside.
Longmans in the '90s, then Maunsel in '18
bought his Glengariff story.

O distant country!
O broken dreams!
For liberation is a valley of disappointment –
after power, the mere excitement of museums.

630.

The past is so rural and intimate, if we forget
the rotted corpse in ditch-water, hooded
and whole streets disembowelled like spineless books.
The past has charm like cut glass or wickerwork:
beware of novelists throwing or weaving that –
Alexander MacArthur's *Irish Rebels* or Lysaght's
Her Majesty's Rebels, their stress of contradictions
like the stress at the apex of heavy thatch.
Their spines have fallen apart, and their stories
withered. Rotted cords, decaying sallie-rods.
They wished to keep two things going at once,
the aesthetic being and the ethnic predicament.
Mr Lysaght, your book is committed to the *worn-out* bin
– like our view of history, from Davis to 1891.

823.BER

The hard cover of this novel comes away in my hand,
the desecrations of time,
like the desecration of farms and great houses
for the common good.
Mr Butler of *The Bad Times* was hauled
into truth, manhandled, as disappointed as Isaac Butt.
For the liberal mind cannot stand violence
as the propertied abhor agrarian unrest –
what is it that we cannot bear to lose?
Binding thread hangs from this damaged book
as corpses hung, feather-like,
from the unpainted gibbet of the nineteenth century.
Our past was in these words, *The Bad Times*
as quiet now as the hanging man without land.

821.LAW

Sweet daughter of our Lord Cloncurry, Emily
Lawless, you wrote *Hurrish* in a hurry
and it flourished for you, for years.
What right did you have to make such fiction
out of death? Was your heart with the Land League?
I'd say not:
no more than the true heart of Longfellow
was in the breast of the Red Indian prince.
Now the world is bleak, by café or lake.
I can only think your mutilated book
is a song like Hiawatha's,
so dark we must eat our fear together.

THE DYING SYNAGOGUE
AT SOUTH TERRACE

Chocolate-coloured paint and the July sun
like a blow-torch peeling off
the last efforts of love:
more than time has abandoned this,
God's abandonment, God's synagogue,
that rose out of the ocean
one hundred years from here.
The peeling paint is an immigrant's
guide to America – lost on the shore
at Cobh, to be torn and scored
by a city of *luftmenshen*,
Catholics equally poor, equally driven.

To have been through everything,
to have suffered everything and left
a peeling door. *Yahweh* is everywhere,
wherever abandonment is needed –
a crow rising after a massacre,
wearing the grey uniform
of a bird of carrion, a badger
waiting for the bones of life
to crack before letting go:
wishing the tenth cantor to die,
the synagogue to become a damp wall,
the wailing mouths to fester.
Too small. To be a small people
aligned to nothing is to suffer blame
like a thief in the night. Some activist
throws a bomb for the suffering PLO:

the sky opens and rains a hail
like snowdrops. Flowers for memory,
petrol for the faraway.

To define one's land is to be a cuckoo
pushing others, bird-like, into a pit,
until at the end every national gesture
becomes painful, soiling the synagogue
door, like the charcoal corpses
at Mauthausen Station, 1944.

We who did nothing for you, who
remained aloof with the Catholic world
and would have cried *Jew!* like the others –
David forgive us –
we who didn't believe the newsreels,
preferring hatred of England to love of you,
we might shut our hypocrite mouths,
we want a West Bank but not a Stormont.
We have no right over your batons,
having made nothing for you but L. Bloom.

To sit here now in the rancid sunshine
of low tide is to interiorize
all of the unnoticed work of love –
exquisite children fall like jewels
from an exhausted colporteur's bag;
a mid-century daughter practises piano,
an *étude* to cancel terror; a nephew
dreams of the artistic life, another
shall practise law and become, in time,
the Catholic's tall Lord Mayor.
Where these jewels fall beside the peeling door
let us place the six lilies of memory;
the six wounds of David's peeling star.

THINKING OF MY FATHER
IN THE MUSÉE PICASSO

It breaks my heart to think of your failures,
for you were not a bad man, just hopeless.
The lost Party, those lethal social forces
that broke your will broke others less poor.
Talent is a muscle that needs constant exercise
and Ireland was your disagreeable milieu –
all the end-of-term banter of the Dáil
couldn't hide that truth. But look at Picasso:
he was a bullish, besieged Stalinist,
yet he worked and worked and worked.
Every butterfly of an idea he embraced became art;
and every false move he made used material
more permanent and beautiful than the Dáil.

PICASSO'S 'COMPOSITION AU PAPILLON'

When I contemplate your magic gifts tonight,
alone, the back-boiler creaking, the frosty moonlight,
I am reminded that you were Leonardo
reincarnate, the Cuchulain of canvas.
Paint never buckled under such pressure –
Guernica, vulgar goats, the portraits of Olga;
even something as brittle as 'Composition au Papillon'
has the finished look to make gods finite.

In Paris, at fifty-one, you could play God
with cloth, string, a thumb-tack, oil. Truth is
we are all born to an artless, provincial stench.
If we are lucky, Picasso, we die French.

HUGH MacDIARMID

Here on the Celtic fringe ice is very thin;
if you speak a word of English I'll fall in,
into the *muckle toon* of florid talk,
the quagmire of manners, the velvet catwalk
of bourgeois courtesy. Let us kiss each other
on the arse for luck, and not stir
again until I've praised as best I can
your own gift, and your genius, Scotland.
How you suffered at the hands of others,
dear Chris! The air was very thin
between cabins, the kirk too full of nerves
to challenge those who came to burn and sin.
Dr Grieve, remember the good luck
of having a postman for a father
and a post-office full of Victorian books
to cheer you while you waited there.
Scotland's past was a parcel of ill-luck,
with you, its covering letter, gone astray.
History can't close on the Sabbath Day,
nor poetry. They festered in the volumes
that you took away. Poor man's child, say
'I'm sorry. I know too much for my age.
My bourgeois teachers are in a rage.'

The sentimental masters would have you praise
our unique Celticness, the infinite
boredom of the picturesque, braes
at break of day. I can hear you say
'What about the slums, the insomniac
nature of poverty and disease?'
You had a continent elsewhere
to write about: Stalin's land
that you and they could barely understand.

As Benedict of Clusa used to say
to the troublesome Bishops of Aquitaine
'I have two houses full of books,
I meditate upon them every day.'

How much of Scotland fell apart
when you broke down, how many mere tits' eggs
that would have pleased the pious kirk?
More natural achievements took their place:
a winter mezereum, differential calculus,
that dragged you into a wider arc
to stare amazed at the mere *material*.
There, on the material fringe, the ice
was very thin. You swallowed more
than Scotland whole when you jumped in.

The Lost Province

THE GARDEN OF SEMPERVIRENS

We've been in this small room since daybreak.
I look out on America, sunlight on the great plain
of a neighbour's roof, an Ojibwa spirit
racing by. We lie at ease for our own sake.
The frenzy of late March or a nineties puritan
need for work can't move us from our perch.
You do move your arm, grown a little numb
from the weight of me. We both talk of home

and how we must go back. But for now
we are as numb as a young prisoner in Portlaoise
who hears these words for the first time, *amnesty*, *ceasefire*.
At five thousand miles we manage somehow
to find a new vocabulary for peace.
Peace, like light, is almost too much to bear.
After so many years, how to come into the sun,
pull the harrow from the brambles, set to garden.

From this bed where we made love I can see
more than a few winter creatures basking in light.
A College mower goes by, but squirrels hang on.
Late March America is theirs completely;
all ten thousand lakes and a thousand islands.
Our own life has the sandalwood vapour of night
marked with the fresh touch of your mouth,
love and story, the accent of the South.

Yet what I might have written was suspended
the way yard-work is in a Minnesota winter.
We held our breath. Now, see the winter heads of Clematis,
the winter colour of *Bergenia*, or *Skimmia*,
with its white panicles of fragrance, up-ended.
We see again the private lust of poems and paralysis
of poetry in a time of war; and how, undeterred,
Buxus keeps its shape, year after year, *in memoriam*.

PRISONS

for Catherine

You walk across the compound on a clear day,
the morning damp with dew –
dawn like a squad-car carrying you
away from me. I watch the way
you walk, elegant as usual,
into the new prison school.

Out of one prison into another.
Last night the determined prison officer, our son,
poked at you with the warm baton
of his bottle, his eight-ounce *Pur*.
There's no escape from the love
he has cast about us, and no reprieve.

You were so free when I first saw you
ten years ago. When you walked
(no woman ever had a walk as bold as yours)
out into sunlight from the pub door,
I hand-cuffed you into talk,
I was your holiday inquisitor.

Embarrassed eyes gave you away.
While others pleaded I held you on remand,
my fingers touching your hand.
You withheld your address. But today,
today, you walk through the new prison gate,
your scarf beside me like a half-sheet.

A NAVY SKIRT

A wet and house-bound day at the end of July:
we meet briefly and kiss
among the coral islands of old clothes.
You are clearing the wardrobe. Life's come to this,

this vital reassessment in the encrusted ocean
of our bedroom. A navy skirt lies on the floor
as it lay years ago near a glass of wine.
A purple tie-dyed blouse is torn

from your life. The scattered black and green kelp
of tops and trousers, frayed sweaters, that were
part of my love for you are helped
into the oblivion of black bags. The shore

is littered with your former selves. Lovers
I touched have been consigned to dust, to sand
and water. I knew your moods by their textures.
Your changing patterns I watched, to understand

which good moment to ask a favour. So much
was granted in the licence of clothes: sex,
a soul to speak with, anecdotes against loneliness.
Now the ocean takes all your polo-necks

and lace collars. The ground is littered
with the left-overs. You've fulfilled the chore
of coming into focus. You offer, again, a brief kiss.
Whole futures surge in to your tidied space.

HERE YOU ARE

Stranded for hours at Belfast Central
I have time to look again and again
at three photographs in my breast pocket.

How fragmentary life is! How powerful
images are that cut into us like shrapnel.
Images push forward against loneliness.

Here is Pasternak, a photograph
brought home from Russia by poet friends:
here – after the riots – is the poet,

all birch trees, cornflowers and carnations.
And here are my two brothers, a small
black and white photograph I took in 1968

or '69. They are playing with a terrier
in the Cistercian field. Kevin is laughing –
the baby, we are proud of his intelligence.

And here you are, lost in contemplation
on a Kerry beach. The sea is behind you,
breaking gently at the centre of my heart.

Your check skirt billows in the wind,
a squall catches your hennaed curls.
This love we carry is a telephoto lens.

HONEYMOON PORTRAIT

What survives is an image of you
as youth on the brink of some new distress.
Neither the raw carnivals of Paris
or *fin de siècle* ironworks break through

to allow for celebration. Your distant
look, your eyes that went dark with boredom,
constantly escape from the cheap bedroom
of tourist art. Your anecdotes rinse

the romantic hogwash out of moonlight.
Wait, who mentioned the moon?
Give the moon a break. The highly strung
Vietnamese exile has a perfect right

to paint the moon or dissolve the moon
to suit the purpose of her loaded brush.
What murderous B-26 crushed
her native studio and made her a Western

portrait painter? She chokes now in the lacquer
factory of Paris. She is one more displaced
woman, bombed out with her mother
from the Asian delta. The chalk she placed

to her lips was sulphurous with napalm.
Between you two there was a resonant mantra:
a prayer excluding men. You shared tourism
of the globe and the female body. I saw

the look of exile in her trapped eyes.
She caught the look of a honeymoon in you:
how no intelligent woman could subdue
the loss of territory that a marriage means.

NOVEMBER

The sun has burned the toast of the morning
yet again. Outside our window, late mist
is blown upriver. A thrush begins to sing;
it spits through the flaky Saturday haze.

In the yard there isn't much left of autumn.
Frayed Virginia leaves in the corner
are the summer's disquieting shrapnel –
one year on, an Arts Council grant winds down.

Life that is fragmentary and difficult
has had space to run with outstretched arms;
the blame and lack of love you might have felt
is deeper now. Our child bawls like an alarm

as he has done every night for two years.
Has he found me wanting? I would not wish him
the father I had; hopeless father
who couldn't shield us from the bitching parish

of his own misery. The house was claustrophobic
but only with his own troubles.
It takes so long for a father to learn love,
to ditch the hero for the outstretched hand.

We survive self-knowledge like the memory
of war or a car crash. Not only ourselves
are victims but those who teach us to love.
Each year vanities fall away like leaves

to expose more of our basic structure,
all lopped branches and cankered scars.
Here is memory, here is the recent humus
of trouble. The new gutter sheds tears.

Each gust of wind traps more retreating leaves,
keeps them cornered, makes a damp imprint
of whatever wound. The full year grieves
like a bomb-victim in a basement

and poems come like ballads of the IRA,
under pressure but not admitting love;
primed to defend the hot selected areas.
There, time stands still, more naked and unkind

as years pass overhead. In the shopping mall
of parenthood we are lost. There are fractious walks
in the park, tired shoulders in a wood
or seaside strolls where once was horny talk

before love-making. These, the recurring images
of you, seashells, stones on a sunlit beach,
dolphins, these come to me at the edge
of autumn. They are out of reach

too often now. Pressure of the domestic,
ritual duties of the house. We yearn for more:
domesticity is only interim music.
Love feeds at the edge beyond the seashore

from where it springs. Leaves brush against
the breakfast window. You are asleep once more
after a night of lustful happiness
stolen from the kids. Let's get a divorce

from them and hide in the foliage. Toast
is burning for you through the breakfast news.
The purple dregs of wine in a glass –
Californian, and ripe as figs

against a November wall – have not lost
their sexual taste. The night was seed-filled
and hot as any night in adolescence.
The deep tannin of love still holds.

Only poetry itself is ever autumnal,
wanting to drag in and to store too much.
Better to lose as much again, overturn creels
of possible images. One cannot store touch

or the sensuous moment. The year hangs
now from the cliff of autumn. Winter fills
us already with its compositions, its strange
cleansing light. Rain has washed window-sills

and left them gasping. The haze has lifted.
I breakfast on the good words between
us now. Winter arrives with its gifted
techniques. Leaf fragments adhere to glass, seem

like marmalade pieces left on a plate
or sweet-papers blown across a beach.
I move to the grill to turn up the heat
for more toast. Sunlight is within reach

if only I could touch the lintel of November.
Familiar smells, the grill-pan warms.
November, your birthday. Love breathes upon fear
the way a kiss moistens an exposed arm.

SNOW

Cold palette of winter on the narrow lane.
I park the fat beige tube of car and walk.
Kate's hair, like a wayward streak of Titian,
cuts through the pure viridian of air.
We jump to avoid the soluble blue
of an Opel, a strong Prussian intruder.
Our hand link across the bismuth white
of packed snow. Without speech,
warm in the encrusted seal of her lips,
we catch the blue of a child hurrying indoors.
A nod of acknowledgement, a thumb raised,
delicate as camel-hair, she disappears.
Suddenly, the brilliant tincture of a child's laugh
from the cuchrome of the cloakroom.

Daughter, your lips are too sore to kiss now;
your cool face, titanium white of inert snow.

AN EXCHANGE OF GIFTS

for Denis

We are here at the edge of the known world,
arriving at Easter to exchange gifts of chocolate.
You have been walking among the medieval laurels
with my wife. The children play on a black gate,

chasing the new watch-dog, inventing names
for things they haven't even touched. Red
of frosted camellia and flowering crab
catch the light. Evening is a watery Pieris.

You talk together as if talking to some part
of me; which is what love is, how it should be.
During these terrible weeks she has been my heart.
A Geraldine officer, you know about anxiety;

territory lost, foreign wars, brothers in trouble.
It is wrong to gain too much at once –
you look back and see things diminish, castle by castle;
just our organic life is left, then nothingness.

We step indoors to exchange small gifts.
Eggs in silver wrapping accumulate.
Still, they are more than good manners. Votive,
they are candles of one kind of faith.

Your mother's carriage-clock chimes. I listen
to its prudent reminders. Wars and fathers
break through the silver-wrap. The children scream
with delight. They gambol across the hours.

Timeless barbarians, they won't behave.
Egg-shaped, noble, life is at the table's edge
while a child goes by. What we are sure of
is memory, with its blue and gold Fabergé.

THE LEINSTER FITZGERALDS

for D.H.F. on his 80th birthday

I know you hate the cult of birthdays –
for yours came at the wrong time of year,
three weeks into a new term,
and all the loneliness of a boarding school.

The trees you've planted have kept your secret:
Amalancier leaf-spears, overflowing Bourbon roses,
colour the page of days into a greeting.
The equinox blows its eighty candles,

quickly the smoke is claimed by the bonfire.
Years open like courtyards at Carton –
your ancestors come onto the terrace to cheer.
There's Emily, the Duchess, and betrothed

in early youth. There's the whipper-snapper
young Jacobite and his Pamela de Genlis;
there, behind her, walking from the farrier's yard,
is the Great Earl himself, and Garret Og.

What a party! No expense is spared.
The trees have put out their best spoons,
the lawn is a broad heraldic carpet.
Birds run through the usual brass tunes.

– And still your day is a secret.
Except in the encumbered estate of the mind:
there, long wax candles burn for you. Your name
is spoken. There's a Humphrey Lyttleton band.

TRISKEL ODEON

Another film-club Saturday. Lights down.
The screen lights up to show its fabric art.
We sit quietly in the Triskel Odeon,
watch a director bare his serious heart

with the heating up too high. There is sweat
already on my buttoned-up shirt.

The projector fulfils its whispered threat
and breaks down. Suddenly dreams fall apart

as quickly as they're projected. I wait,
with one hundred other adults, for noise
and light to begin again. At this rate
we'll never have our weekend blast, our money's

worth of foreign films and sin.
We shift uneasily in our directors' chairs;
wisecracks, as diffuse as light through muslin,
fill the air. It's back again! There's

a rush of sunlight, the healing Mediterranean.
If only our small towns could have been like that;
if we could rearrange and splice the frames
to make a new milieu, begin with something white

instead of sleet on St Patrick's Day, or Fianna Fail.
Someone blew the projector bulb of our childhood,
leaving a wet, grey street. No *Amarcord*
to talk about, no olive trees; no cinematic light.

DESMOND CINEMA, CAPPOQUIN

I sit with John Crowley in the projection room
of McCarthy's ambitious Desmond Cinema.
There is the flapping sound of a reel's end
that John has been rewinding for return.

It may be a film from Paramount
like *We're No Angels* or *To Catch a Thief*
(I think it was Cary Grant's face
that passed us by on a damaged frame).

John has been here since before I came
into the undirected world of waste and death.
Cappoquin, 1960. He's projected light
over the heads of those left in town –

their bodies writhing under the higher etiquette
of Hollywood as well as Church and State.
I wish I could unreel the many sounds
that lulled our backwater of happiness:

the silver tones of Nelson Eddy's throat,
the weak-kneed mush of *GI Blues*,
the alarming hooter in *How Green Was My Valley*,
and music from *The Song of Bernadette*

that haunted mothers who couldn't emigrate.
John, spools click in the empty auditorium.
You strap tightly the aluminium film box,
send dreams like emigrants on the 4 o'clock train.

THE NEW EURO-ROAD

Election posters in the winter rain. The car
like a magic carriage brings me back –
attendant mice, rodent footmen –
roads tending clockwise in the winter clock,

time won't run out until we get back.
Rain falls in the principality of brown cows.
Rain cascades from the luggage rack.
Water has primed the November hedgerows.

We can never get back to the first surface of home.
From the new EC road – raised above flood-level

with German money – I can see the river-side street
where I was born. I can hear the church bells.

The town cowers like an exhausted father.
Everything has changed. We were never closer to Bonn,
or Milan or Cologne. We were never closer
to a fairy tale. Heartbroken afternoons at home

now seem like details from another biography.
My past has the texture of an Italian film:
to be seen fully certain blinds must be drawn down
against the light, and talk kept to a minimum.

Misfortune flooded my childhood so many times.
It's good to see it now from a raised Euro-road.
Would I go back? Would a donkey go back to the mines?
Would a salmon return to a lake without food?

POLLING DAY, 1989

Another hot day at the end of the campaign;
not a crowd to fill my punishment-cell library
or the distant tennis-club polling station.
I lunch in the shade of an ugly sycamore tree

and watch the drying straws of a late June.
A Green Party van chugs by, emphysemic,
rattling in the potholes of our Republic.
A Fine Gael woman walks from her blue BMW

to show clothes any mortal would vote for.
She is tanned with the confidence of her class,
gifted, walking with purpose. A red Labour poster
vies with the black-rimmed borders

of Sinn Fein. A government car
speeds by, raising dust in the blistered street;
its tinted occupant is blissfully unaware
of sycamore, dying library or summer heat.

I finish my sandwich and fold the cellophane
of my lunch-hour into a tight ball. The hard
mahogany of the bookshelves beckons. No rain;
sycamores drop their unwanted polling-cards.

THE COUNT CENTRE

Once again, the aleatory ballot-box.
Franchise clerks tumble dice across the table.
Power has broken its seal.

Trestle-tables are loaded with wads of votes;
candidates chew their Cuban pencils.
There's a call for order.

This is the tense time of dealing out –
a tallyman grumbles quietly, a clerk
moves away to make room for lamplight.

The tables are littered with wild returns,
a shift of emphasis, a weird transfer.
Eyes strain to see what an opponent has.

Hard necks are stretched.
This day is beyond us, beyond words.
All, at once, are triumphant, wretched.

THE WAITING DEPUTIES

Tonight I drive through my native county.
Ten o'clock, all the canvassing over,
the lights go out in the last polling booth.
Incumbents await their final transfer.
What is it that my childhood meant to say,
I wonder? Just one version of the truth

will out tomorrow when seals are broken.
I drive through the latest interregnum
as November rain drove through here for weeks.
Posters lie torn in the exhausted towns
of Dungarvan and Lismore. The rain-storm
of polling day has abated. The night speaks

to me like an old detective –
it protects the boxes and seals power.
Who will be responsible for my childhood
when the votes are counted? Where
will the blame fall? The way I live
now prevents any party from looking good:

what I write, remember and feel
excludes me from their well-connected world.
When I was poor these men did business
as if nothing happened. I was told
they had power to attend to: they used to sail
in and out of our demented terrace.

The unopened boxes will see me right.
My parish sleeps on its pillow of votes.
Cappoquin, between river and the trees,
ignores its grumbling questioner, its poet.
It sleeps upon favours. In the calm of night
they wait with me, the would-be Deputies.

SNAP ELECTION

The Party men have failed you in three colours.
A councillor tells stories. You sit beside him
in desolation. It is the spring of 1973.
You bend your head like a jilted lover.
Television light flickers across the room;
a neon hunchback with a threatening broom
that spits upon you and empties ash-trays.
It repeats figures and mentions the weather.

You move your legs reluctantly and brood.
Never blame a higher power, never.
It's the local district that brings failure.
You moved in the small arena, three townlands
at most, and no more expected help from Dublin
than from Christ. There are Party men you loathe
who failed to deliver the budding votes.
You bind the voters' lists in an elastic band

and raise your whiskey to a term without power.
A more hostile Dáil will eat your liver.
Death will catch you in its snap election
before the decade ends. Provoked by television
you walk away into the post-election rain,
avoiding candidates – the four failed names
as if they had committed some crime against you,
a bleak betrayal of family, a desecration.

POLLING DISTRICTS

Midsummer thunder has made the sky clear –
lounging clouds have been for a long walk.
The skylight picks out abandoned registers,
shredded by the teeth of years. Pencil-marks
of young personation officers start
to burn off in the light. A Tupperware
jar of indelible pens is canvassed
by a party of spiders, a microphone of chalk
breaks through to dominate the plastic soapbox.

Sunlight gnaws the floorboards where they lie,
dusty now and naked, and dog-eared.
So much power has gone quiet; its weird
and remarkable loss is a mystery.
I can almost hear the pages cry
although the attic-boards creak and resist
any perfect silence. Crouched low, I try
to arrange old polling districts in a neat
pile. Pages are smudged with my father's sweat.
I think of his red hand on those voters' lists,

a hand that was absent so often from our house.
He had to canvass too many other places,
neighbourhood terraces, walls for notices,
not to mention drunken election crowds.
But these abandoned registers, the lost quires
in our attic, are my keepsakes for 1977.
Nothing less than his indices of heaven,
they decay more quickly every passing year.

SHROUD

The Taoiseach's face comes into grey focus
like the lately usurped Turin Shroud.
His speech is barely audible. The distress
of failure cannot be hidden from the crowd.

Crumbs are thrown at the gasping press corps;
images to fill up the emptiness of days,
gossip to feed that hunger. Running scared
at the nothing in our lives, we praise

a photographer's tit-bit. Flashbulbs tell us
what we already know. It's been a tough
campaign; power has suffered a hair-loss,
the Taoiseach is ill, tired, becoming rough

with those who question or disagree.
The helicopter gunships of the canvass
have left unbearable ringing in his ears;
a cynical decompression has taken place.

A bulb flashes like a fresh blood-stain.
What is it that keeps him going?
Is it power only? The sacred? The Shroud of Turin
that fills our man with the Jesus thing?

Is it that some Deputy might touch the hem
of his Government and become important,
or some dark Magdalene
wipe perspiration from his face. Can years

of anxiety fall away? Photographers hint
at nothing more than mortal grace, his tiredness.
Television, our daily linen, leaves a quick imprint.
Elected Christs disappear without trace.

MICK HANNIGAN'S BERLIN WALL

Your wall, Mick, fragmentary and dry
like a crust of burned soda bread,
has travelled across the snowy American
country. Your wall has become my daily bread:
more real and sacred
than a piece of the True Cross could be,

and more transcendental than poetry.
Daily I go to the Communion of plaster
and feel its stinging flakes.
I wonder how many demolished homes
went into its making; the holy sepulchre
of Berlin torn apart and emptied

to be reconstructed as a mere wall,
a miserable, miserable wall. One people
were divided and terrified. It was, someone said,
their just punishment –
as our divided island is a just thing:
perfect image of the spirit unwilling.

Mick, I divided your wall in Syracuse.
No, not Syracuse. It was Burlington, Vermont.
I gave it to a poet during a snowstorm.
A divided Sacred Host. I thought guilt
and history are divisible like Grace.
He thanked me as one thanks a priest.

THE LOST PROVINCE OF ALSACE

I   SPEECH

That June afternoon, drinking near Grafton Street
after your father's speech in the Dáil,
we fell into conversation
with two Catholic girls from Tyrone.
Their fingernails were still lightly chipped
from hanging off the ledge of the North.
They were full of emigré hope and gratitude.
They had both landed jobs in the capital.

I mentioned the Beef Tribunal, the 'golden circle',
the ten-year betrayal of the unemployed.
They would have none of it.
Dublin had opened and they had season tickets.
It was you who mentioned the old Senator
in the Dreyfus affair, Sheurer–Kestner –
after 1871 he chose to live in France
but kept his eyes open, read all the documents:
in this way never lost the province of Alsace.

II   NATIONAL TREACHERY

Our neighbour's son, a teacher's oldest child,
lay down beside me in Deputy Glenville's field.
We spent whole days looking at the sky,
wondering what held it up, wondering why

it was always blue. He became so concerned
about the sky that he fell seriously ill.
Professionals counselled him through the term.
He avoided me when he came out of hospital.

The big questions never troubled me as a child.
Questions dissolved inside me like vitamins.
I fed upon them. I was solitary and spoilt.
Yet there was one recurring question: it burned

a hole in my heart. Afraid to ask friends,
it went unanswered. I'm alone with it still.
Why was my father powerless, and all my cousins?
What treachery did we commit against the Dáil?

III   CITY OF ROSES

The people who were happy with Stormont
loved roses, or so you insisted.
You travelled north in late '64
to sell steel gates to men who wore
metal Union Jacks in their lapels.
Lemass's voice was ringing in your ears:
'If thine eye offend thee, do business.'
There were MacGredy roses everywhere you went.
It was a city of roses, it was.
You bought two H.T.s for your married lover,
hid them like contraceptive devices.
Long after, their grit stuck to your clothes;
and bits of a wet *Newsletter* that covered
their thorns, their hybrid Talmudic pages.

IV   AT PORTLAOISE PRISON, 1993

It is time for the lighting of lamps,
sancte venite, the coming of night.
Portlaoise prison, custodial hands
are placed upon ceramic light.

Republicans retire into their cells,
certain I have left unfinished
the long ambiguity of poems.
I leave the scriptorium, a list

of scholars and heroes in my notes.
Gracious, the monks have given me a gift
of tooled leatherwork.
Generous they are, even as they resist

the flux of liberal ideas:
they give what it is their minds make.
The monastic code is precious.
Their view of history is what takes

some time to understand. It lacks
a medieval world. For poets may come,
luminous with ambiguity,
gifted as *filí*, welcoming Englishmen.

V   TALKING TO GERRY ADAMS, 1994

We are three floors above your foot-soldiers,
which is the right of those who exchange ideas.
We know nothing about fuses:
we detonate opinions and views.
Your handsome face (the face of an IRA man
in Keating's *Men of the South*), has no pain
visible to me. It has absorbed politics,
and flying columns of documents.

Today it's the 'productive atmosphere of peace'
after war. I find myself switching sides
already. Maybe this is what poets are for
in a destitute time. To stay apart
from the Dáil. Thinking finds a Protestant in me;
and Ulster, an autonomous region of the heart.

If it was a train only, it wasn't
at this small station

It was one of those five afternoons
in Paradise. A bone-dry day,
nettles and parsley on the embankment.
A train pulled out of Cappoquin Station.

The earth moved, and the train
like an elephant spitting through the trees
beat me from the ticket office. Was it
Jackie Greene, the phlegmatic clerk,

who flagged it back again?
I can't remember. But I recall my foot
on the grey, moulded pedal-step
and the feel of a master's hand at my back

pushing me on. The August afternoon
carried me drunk to Dungarvan.
Even then I knew I'd used one day
out of the four or five in childhood.

It is risky and primitive, it is
an unhappy childhood

Images of grief take time to be formed.
Only now I've learned to handle our father,
his meticulous, minutely organized idleness.
He stood in our childhood corridor,
a depressed face-painter, painting stress-
lines. Our mother, busy and inarticulate,
looked on as we queued to be crayoned.

Yet he had such sweetness of character –
how many times did our mother fall asleep
in his arms? He held up the tent of the night
with his stories. He triggered our mother's laugh.
Sometimes her laugh was heard on the street.
Their love was clairvoyant and deep:
nothing that happened could touch it,

not even us. A day went by in their life,
it was only one day, it was risky and primitive
as love is a chance and a bond
that gives the weak courage. One day a wife
walks indoors with her strange new husband:
who knows what ghost will touch their lives?
Fate will hold them in the palm of its hand;

it will blow upon them, cold air
from the letter-box, furnace of the bedroom.
Still, their crises primed us with feverish hands;
them licking crayons for our hearts' thin paper.
Depression was an art-supplier.
Their memory is a tcar-based pigment. Words form,
again and again, to speed its aphaeresis.

It is poems I bring to assuage his melancholy,
anecdotes from the bourgeois life

Your father gazes steadily through the window.
The world looks in at him and guesses.
Melancholy has given him a peculiar foothold:
books wash quietly from the bourgeois world.

They settle at his feet. Ah, he has just missed the boat,
just by half a government. If he'd been in the Party then,
if his intelligence had learned to negotiate,
he might have come home to a political welcome.

Instead, he is powerless in his working-class island.
Reading has set him apart. He doesn't understand
that books are like dead voters, an embarrassment.
Melancholy has gripped his beautiful, trapped heart.

Believe me, it's worse to witness anger
than to meet it head on. It's more like fiction

The sun on impulse lifts above Cappoquin, throws
light upon your father's endogenous depression.
It is middle-age in the adult world.
Sunlight falls upon the libido of trees

and sets the world chattering, chattering.
Birds, like so much grain, lift from the weighty earth,
become a shower skywards. The kettle is singing
in the mother-lit fireplace. Your mother

has risen at dawn to be before you.
Her steady gaze now is what holds us together.
Gone the happy politics, the health of friendship.
He is no more a man, but the absence of one.

Your eyes are on the light from the window,
the morning paper-round, obligations made clear.
You leave the house, but your mother has still to listen.
She grumbles quietly in the district of fear.

I think of the fathers I've invented,
and marvel that the earth is calm

I watch from my father's meadow
the outgathering of swallows.
They mince the light afternoon –
a ratatouille of shadows
oiled by the falling sun.
Autumn flings them across trees and wires,
specks of life go lighter and higher
until snuffed by the peregrine

of distance. The earth is more calm.
It's immovable, even warm
compared to cold ideas in the sky.
A rock-rose comes to little harm
down here, a scandent jasmine, white-eyed,
feeds off the last humus of summer.
Petals heave at the least murmur.
August settles old scores at my side.

Here things are different and the same:
different since our children came
and moved us back a generation.
Being in the world is less pain
since they waved their mystical arms.
Ideas are no longer migrant
only, but rooted to the land
that constitutes their names.

It's love that marched them through the trees
to check engines that might have ceased –
too many ideas, cloudbursts, rains,
rusted life, left us diminished.
Sunnier now the wear and tear
that calms my dread, implosive anger.
Their fragrance falls across our knees.

I watch more swallows bank southward.
Early evening still, the air is cold
already. Michaelmas stretch their green fists
from the Senecio carpet. Untold
stories lodge in the pampas grass.
From here I can hear their gossip;
watch politicians take malicious shape,
each pulled by the tropism of disgrace.

I think of the terrible mistake poets made
who attached themselves
to Marx instead of their fathers.
Laws of light and leaves
cannot be altered. Green corridors
of natural law never submit.
Philosophy bends to sunlight
and seasons. Earth is umbilical of power;

and nothing so puritan, so man-made,
as dialectical secateurs
can sever the bond with the dead.
And this belongs to all. Others,
behind whichever Balkan wall,
often luxuriate in loss.
I recall Bloody Sunday. You recall
Enniskillen. Corpses lie on our flowers

while we think and talk and watch.
We marvel at the conference of swallows.
I gather a few myrtle logs
from your winter pile of lime and larch.
Their bark is the colour of blood
myrtle cut from its natural home
and left to die. Through it, be understood
the ironic warmth of the war poem.

It is Stormont, it is the Dáil
that makes an awkward, distant Hell-
place where swallows go to browse.
Truth is only a kind of petal
blown against the wall of each house.
It is power, it is powerful men
I've interiorized. They leave me troubled
and uprooted in my father's garden.

DECLAN, SCIENTIST

Super aegros imponent manus et bene habebunt

I   BBC GAUL

The sea lives in constant amazement
with itself. Our grey promontory,
our business park that natives call
the monastery, or monastic settlement,

can never outshine the sea.
Its harvest is welcome but tragic.
Even I myself have felt
(like followers of the Patrick cult)

the sea's desperate loneliness.
Were it not for the radio at night –
BBC Gaul, Fluctus-Brevis News, Radio Lux –
I might become a wind-torn anchorite.

II   THE HEATHEN GODS

Today we learned about the heathen Gods,
gods of water and earth. But especially Brigid,
a kind of foundress Mary Baker Eddy,
whose cloak of prayer covered acreage

bigger than our business enclosure.
God showed displeasure through her
with boils and sores. The land reveals itself
thus, layer by infected layer.

III FALL

Leaves scatter in our healing park.
Wind blows the untreated parchment
of summer. The stripped bark
from our charcoal fires
flutters in the west wind.

Another summer as Christ's instrument.
Time flies. Twenty little gurriers
are rescued from the Patrick cult.
Clear signals on the 30m band
and these, psalms on all four winds,
Fall's blessed diatesseron.

IV FEATHERS

The teeming bird–life of the Patrick cult:
all these blackbirds of the enclosure
like the tears of octopus on parchment,
loathsome Celtic ousel and robin.
The elder Julius has been up since dawn
laying down poison:

such a cloudburst of the feathered dead!

V GALILEE

Not for us the bleak last supper
of the suffering Patrick cult,
rather the joyous morning picnic
with the risen Christ as exemplar.

We are flattered by Princes of the Deisi
bearing gifts; filigree gold
for melting down to micro-chips,
complicated Pictish MSS

and a white-haired Princess.
We gaze upon this beautiful daughter
of an unsaved Celtic chieftain –
gold nor God-health will move her.

VI   MOCHUDA

I pray for Brother Mochuda's wound.
It festers and grieves in him.
Pain is more than a memory with him
since he fell from the short-wave aerial.

God be good to Mochuda
who tried his best to receive news from Gaul
on the thirty-metre band.
Mochuda, native Gael, you broke your back

while searching for God. The elders
love you. All the elders from Cappoquin
have prayed over you. Even the wind howls;
your radio mast takes the strain.

VII   AD 435, AUGUST

Another day of aching heat –
grass high and stiff as a donkey's rod,
the sea a looking-glass.
Brother Mochuda's been sharing God
with Patrick's victims.
Alas, there's hardly grain or meat
enough for a healing colony.

'Brother,' I said, 'I know it's August
and the first roots will soon be lifted,
but there are too many mouths to feed.
Why don't you return to the broadcast Christ.
Radio has such influence . . . Just for a month.
DXers have less physical needs.'

XIII   LOVE

More dynastic quarrels in the North.
A pall of smoke is visible on Sliabh Gua.
How unlike happiness smoke is,
how it contains a false warmth of fire.

Mochuda has been pining for the fair-haired
Princess. He suffers. He has fallen
into that malicious animal magnetism.
We have been praying against his grief,

this woman who has ensnared him.
But he seems not to want relief.
All day he looks north to the *Rian Bó Phadráig* –
erotic ambush on his damaged brain.

IX   BOSTONIUM

Come in! Come in!

It's the Mother Church, Bostonium.
Brother Mochuda is frantic for news.
The waveband, narrow as gallium arsenide,
is difficult to hold. 'Don't lose
us!' he yells from the scriptorium.

Poor Mochuda. He fades. Last night
he saw a young woman bathed in light.

X   ST DECLAN'S STONE

A minor prince refuses to see the light.
'You!' he screams at me 'are people of no background!'

Their genealogies are full of horse-shit –
as if a man were no better than his birth:

M. Rosa,
M. Nair,
M. Fiachair,
M. Conaill,
M. Mecar,
M. Oengusa.

When I came over the sea from Gaul
on a boulder of coarse gritstone
I came with one father only, Christ.
The well-begot comforter.

INDEX OF TITLES

Some Recent Poetry from Anvil

Heather Buck
Waiting for the Ferry

Nina Cassian
Take My Word for It

Peter Dale
Edge to Edge
SELECTED POEMS

Dick Davis
Touchwood

Carol Ann Duffy
The World's Wife
LIMITED EDITION

Time's Tidings (ed.)
GREETING THE 21ST CENTURY

Martina Evans
All Alcoholics Are Charmers

Michael Hamburger
Collected Poems 1941–1994
Late

Donald Justice
Orpheus Hesitated Beside the Black River
NEW AND SELECTED POEMS 1952–1997

Marius Kociejowski
Music's Bride

Peter Levi
Reed Music

Gabriel Levin
Ostraca

Stanley Moss
Asleep in the Garden
NEW AND SELECTED POEMS

Dennis O'Driscoll
Weather Permitting
POETRY BOOK SOCIETY RECOMMENDATION

Sally Purcell
Fossil Unicorn

Peter Russell
The Elegies of Quintilius

Peter Scupham
Night Watch

Ruth Silcock
A Wonderful View of the Sea

Daniel Weissbort
What Was All the Fuss About?